THE KAZAKHS
CHILDREN OF THE STEPPES

MAP OF KAZAKHSTAN

The Kazakhs

CHILDREN OF THE STEPPES

by

Chokan and Murat Laumulin

Translated by Simon Hollingworth

Photographs by Pavel Mikheev

GLOBAL ORIENTAL

THE KAZAKHS
CHILDREN OF THE STEPPES
by Chokan and Murat Laumulin

First published 2009 by
GLOBAL ORIENTAL LTD
PO Box 219
Folkestone
Kent CT20 2WP
UK

www.globaloriental.co.uk

ISBN 978–1–905246–99–1

British Library Cataloguing in Publication Data
A CIP catalogue entry for this book is available
from the British Library

Set in Bembo 11 on 12 pt by IDSUK (DataConnection) Ltd
Printed and bound in England by CPI Antony Rowe, Chippenham, Wilts

In Loving Memory of our Mother – Kira Davletgalieva

Contents

In Place of a Foreword: In the Centre of Eurasia

Modern Kazakhstan, located at the very centre of the great Eurasian continent, is a country where diverse and at times contradictory phenomena have synthesized and become intertwined. This is a country that leans both to the East and the West. The rudiments of a nomadic life-style, dating back to ancient times, stand side by side with advanced space programmes. The broadly-accepted high-society way of life does not diminish the Islamic heritage in Kazakh history, which is represented by a great variety of monuments in the south of the country. The geographical, cultural and linguistic features of northern Kazakhstan are a stark reminder of how close Siberia is from here. In the west, Kazakhstan meets the world's largest lake, the Caspian Sea, while to the east it adjoins Asia's grandest mountain system – the Altay Mountains.

The country is populated by many different peoples and cultures. In the course of a history that has been far from simple, Kazakhstan has acquired unique characteristics by virtue of its enterprising and resilient communities which still remember the traditional values of collectivism. Their principal features are tolerance and openness. Each generation and each social group in Kazakhstan prize their personal experience and have their own values: the older generation draws strength from the nomadic tradition and ancient culture; the middle generation relies on its knowledge and excellent education, for which it has the Soviet system to thank. Young people are turning more and more to the West: they are fluent in European languages, they imbibe democratic values and make wide use of the Internet.

From 2006, thanks to the distinctive brand of humour of the British comedian Sacha Baron Cohen, Kazakhstan, at least in name, is no longer a country completely unknown to the rest of the world. This style of humour is directed at many different targets, yet all with no bearing on the real Kazakhstan. And the real Kazakhstan is the focus of this book.

Although Kazakhstan is historically and culturally a part of Central Asia, it is in fact a country lying at the very heart of geographical Eurasia. Residents of Kazakhstan class themselves equally as living in Asia and Europe. Indeed, a considerable part of Kazakhstan (in European terms), the size of the Benelux countries combined, lies in geographical Europe. And yet there are other criteria, too, which enable the Kazakh people to associate themselves with Europe. We will cover these in more detail later in the book.

Kazakhstan is considered to be a very rich country in terms of the resources that lie beneath its surface. In Soviet times it was customary to speak of the entire Periodic Table being available in Kazakhstan. Some added in those days that if certain elements were missing, they could always be created in nuclear reactors, thereby suggesting the huge scientific potential of this Soviet republic. Today Kazakhstan may also compete with the largest grain and meat producers on the planet. Nature has been kind in the diversity it has bestowed on the land. Lost within this enormous country are endless steppes, imposing mountain peaks, beautiful oases and flowering valleys, deserts, Martian landscapes, major industrial cities and homely farmsteads.

However, the most valued possession of the country is not what is found in Nature, despite the incredible extent to which it has influenced the development of the population. Kazakhstan's greatest wealth is its people. The national character of the residents of the country has been moulded under the impact of many factors, including geography, religion and culture, although the greatest influence came from radical changes in the ancient and more recent history of Kazakhstan. The last revolution of this kind occurred not so long ago, in 1991, with the collapse of the grand Soviet socialist empire, of which Kazakhstan was a part. A new Kazakh identity is now actively taking shape which we will cover in detail below.

Thus, through this introduction to Kazakhstan, a country at the heart of Eurasia, our readers may judge for themselves the area of most interest to them, be it the natural world, culture, history or the people. We believe that direct contact is better than information received sight unseen. Nevertheless, to avoid disappointment, to obtain a balanced view, to save time and even to fall in love with the country, our sincere hope is that this book will play its part in achieving such aspirations while reflecting the great diversity that is the Kazakhstan of yesterday and today.

CHOKAN AND MURAT LAUMULIN
Spring 2009

1

The Breath of History

WHO ARE THE KAZAKHS?

Although Kazakhs were little known to the outside world until relatively recently, their name has been on European tongues at the very least since the eighteenth century, albeit in distorted form. From *Kazaks* (or *Kozaks* in the 'Ukrainianized' version) came the term *Cossacks*, the free-roaming warriors of the steppes, who spread terror with their warmongering. The Cossacks were then taken into the service of the Russian Empire and it is from here that they became known to the West. They spoke in a Russian dialect and professed Christianity.[1]

But those from whom the Eastern European Cossacks adopted their name, many customs, military organization, vocabulary, manner of speaking and fighting, that is, the genuine Kazakhs, were a completely different people, and different they remain to this day. Our narrative is devoted to these people, who now attract universal attention owing to the size of their country, their natural riches, extraordinary economic successes and, most importantly, their unique national character, a fusion of Turkic-Islamic culture, steppe traditions and post-Soviet mentality.

There can be no doubt that Kazakhs, in their origins, are 'children of the steppes'. The steppe and the nomadic life-style have left a lasting mark on their ideas, their language, customs and behaviour. Even today, the descendants of the nomads, who settled in the towns and cities in their third and fourth generations, yearn for the limitless space of the steppe. Look into the eyes of your Kazakh

[1] The situation is more or less the same as with the name 'Franks', which moved from a purely Germanic tribe to the Romanic-speaking French.

companion and this yearning will be easy to see. Only do not look too long, else he may recall the warring past of his ancestors.

Archaeologists have identified the remains of about 200 Neolithic settlements, spread over the entire territory of Kazakhstan. In the mid-second millennium BCE this was a place for the mining and processing of copper and bronze. Residents of the region at this time were either tilling the land or rearing livestock. In the first millennium BCE the nomadic tribes arrived on the scene. The third century BCE saw new, Proto-Turkish groups of nomadic livestock farmers, who changed the basically Iranian culture of the local population.

So, over some two or three millennia, events have unfolded in the space now occupied by modern Kazakhstan, which have consequently defined the face of the modern world. At least this is what Kazakhs believe, and do not try to convince them otherwise. It was here that man first tamed the horse and saddled it. It was here that the first proto-nomads broke away from their agrarian brothers and turned to a warring, nomadic way of life. It was here where the ancestors of the Kazakhs first smelted iron and wrought terror with their weaponry on bronze-sword-wielding enemies, from China to Rome. It was here that men's trousers and stirrups for horse-riding were invented.

It was here that great hordes of warring nomadic tribes were born and grew in strength; it was from here that they stormed the Great Wall of China and the city fortifications of Byzantium, Rome, Baghdad and Damascus. At different times the terrified residents of countries where they settled gave them different names: Sakas, Huns, Turks, Kipchaks, Oguz and Tatars, but modern-day Kazakhs see them all as their anthropological ancestors.

It is thought that the ancient ancestors of the Kazakhs and other pastoral peoples of Central Eurasia spoke in languages of the Persian group. One can still find roots of words in the Kazakh language which relate them to other Indo-European peoples: Iranian, Germanic and Slavic. Remote ancestors of the Kazakhs were closer in appearance to Europeans than they were to Mongoloids, as many archaeological finds demonstrate. Yet over time, with the growing demographic expansion of the Turkic tribes from Altai to Siberia, the language, external appearance, customs and culture of the local tribes came to change irrevocably. The language became Turkic,[2]

[2] It is also called Altaic, i.e. Turko-Mongol.

the external appearance Mongoloid, meaning more Asiatic in expression, the customs changed to display greater solidarity and organization.[3] Just one thing remained unchanged – their warring nature.

A new nation, the Turkic people, formed many states in the centre of Eurasia, many great steppe confederations and empires from the fifth to the fifteenth centuries. These khaganates and hordes had different names, but the Kazakh steppe was always there, in the centre of their territory. The greatest shock for Eurasia was the formation of the Mongol Empire, stretching from the Pacific Ocean to the Arctic Ocean, from the Black Sea to the Mediterranean Sea, from Korea to Trieste and from Siberia to Mesopotamia. By the Mongol era, the chroniclers of the time already knew the names of all the tribes that were to make up the Kazakh nation. These tribes were to come from both among the opponents of the Mongols as well as those who contributed to their military power. By the time they were making incursions into Europe, ninety-five per cent of the Mongol army was already comprised of these tribes, whose camps were located in Kazakhstan and southern Siberia.

Soon the Turkic tribes were able to rid themselves of Mongol rule, but by this time irreversible changes had taken place: from Chinggis Khan[4] and the Mongols they inherited political organization, ruling dynasties and the principles of economic and political management. This is how the Kazakh nation was born.[5]

In the course of many wars, conflicts, annexations and transformations in the early fifteenth century, some of the tribes were able to break away from the main Uzbek horde and in the region of modern-day Alma-Ata,[6] in Semirechie, they formed their own Khanate,

[3] Some Turkic tribes, the Kipchaks in particular, retained this external appearance right up to the thirteenth century. There may be times when foreign visitors meet Kazakhs whose external appearance reminds them of their distant Caucasian ancestors.

[4] Commonly known as Genghis Khan

[5] And again, a parallel comes to mind: after Chinggis Khan, only a representative (even if only formally) of a dynasty of Chinggisids he had created could rule in Eurasia. We see a similar picture in Medieval Europe, where only descendants of Charlemagne had the legitimate right to rule.

[6] Known today as Almaty, but to many Kazakhs, the original name of Alma-Ata is used more fondly.

which, as a consequence, was given the name Kazakhskoe, and the tribes that joined the Khanate came to be known as Kazakhs.[7] Very soon they emerged from the narrow framework of Semirechie, uniting dozens of tribes and clans around them, who adopted the general name 'Kazakh', while retaining their tribal identity.

Thus, in the mid-fifteenth century several tribal groupings were formed on the territory of Mogulistan, between Transoxiania and Lake Balkhash, the heart of what later became known as the Kazakh Khanate. The classical Kazakh society (from the sixteenth to the nineteenth centuries) was based on a nomadic way of life, customary law (the Adat) and Islamic legislation (the Shariat). Livestock farming remained the principal occupation. The Kazakh Khanate was divided into three major parts: the Great, the Middle and the Small Zhuzes, or Hordes. A feature of traditional Kazakh society was its structural hierarchy, based on tribal- and clan-based organization, including an aristocracy, commoners and the clergy.

The Kazakhs were ruled by the Khan and the sultans, who had raised their genealogy to the status of 'Great Master of the Universe', that is, to Chinggis Khan. To the surprise of the majority of the Kazakhs' neighbours in Central Asia and in the Middle East (possibly with the exception of the Great Mongol dynasty which ruled in India and the rulers of the Eastern European khanates, which had conquered Russia) they lost this dynastic continuity. Most surprising is that it was even lost by the Mongols themselves. Once they had moved to Buddhism in its lamaistic form, they little resembled the earlier, warring Mongols of the Chinggis Khan era. For this reason the Kazakh sultans were welcome (but sometimes unwelcome) guests of the emirates, sultanates and khanates, where thrones had become vacant. That is why offshoots of the Kazakh Chinggisids ruled from the Crimea to Kashgar.

In the sixteenth and seventeenth centuries, the Kazakhs were confronted with rivals, who dreamed of resurrecting the Mongol Empire in its primordial form. These were the western Mongol Oirat tribes, or the Jungar,[8] who attacked the Kazakh Muslims and

---

[7] The term 'Kazakh' in the steppe meant a vagrant or a dissenter, but the Kazakhs attached a proud, martial meaning to the name.

[8] The Kazakhs called them Kalmyks, and it is under this name that they are known in Russia and Europe.

attempted to capture their towns, oases, mountain pastures and steppe expanses. Historic tradition and the history books assert that there was a time when the threat of physical extermination hung over the Kazakhs.

However, history saw to it that it was the Jungars, who had forced the Kazakhs out into the mountains of modern-day Xinjiang, who were almost totally wiped out; epidemics and the swords of the new rulers of China, the Manchus, did their work. The Kazakhs were able to recover their breath and began reinstated a functioning economy. Very soon they understood that there was more to be gained in trading livestock than there was in conquering and surrounding oneself in the tributes of settled peoples. The Kazakhs quickly adapted to being neighbours with Russia, which became their principal market for the sale of livestock, leather and wool.

In just one century these nomadic warriors were transformed into peaceful shepherd folk and, in the nineteenth century, Russia, having suppressed several bloody rebellions, annexed the Kazakh steppes into its own territory. As a pretext for conquering this land, St Petersburg used the fact that the most bellicose and wholly insubordinate tribes of western Kazakhstan were continuing to live off forays and slave trading, supplying subjects of the Russian Empire to the slave markets of Khiva, Bukhara, Tehran, Istanbul and Cairo.

Russia used the Kazakh steppe as a base for this military invasion of Central Asia and, following the British, they came to call it Turkestan. Very soon the Russian forces came up against the British in Afghanistan and the Chinese in Xinjiang. A major geopolitical battle ensued, known these days as 'The Great Game' thanks to the good graces of the American journalist Eugene Schuyler.[9] At the time, the Kazakhs did not suspect that the Russians had drawn them into a major geopolitical game, as a result of which, in 1991, they came to have the world's third largest arsenal of nuclear weapons. But for now this was a long way off and the Kazakhs were happy to participate in the Russians' military expeditions against other 'infidels', agreeing for itself an immunity, however, in the event of a war between Russia and Turkey, which was headed by the

[9] Certain political scientists, Zbigniew Bzhezinsky in particular, believe that 'The Great Game' was resurrected after the fall of the Soviet Union.

sultan, who as we know was simultaneously the Caliph, the ruler of all true believers.

In 1916, during the Great War in Europe, the Russians ignored this agreement, when Turkey was fighting on the side of the Austrian-German bloc. As a result of the call-up of Kazakhs into the fighting army, a major rebellion ensued, leading to the collapse of colonial power a year before the Great Russian Revolution.[10] This episode prompts us to recall the role of Islam in Kazakh life.

By an irony of fate, the Kazakhs were always seen by their more devout neighbours as poor Muslims. The Kazakhs, like their ancestors thousands of years before them, believed in the spirits of their ancestors and holy shrines, the Sun and the Sky, that is, what is seen in Arabia as paganism. Today, the Kazakhs continue to cultivate pre-Islamic cults, with little regard for what Riyadh thinks of the matter. At the end of the eighteenth century, the Russian Empress Catherine II, although a protestant in origin who had switched to orthodoxy, having heard much about the weak piety of the Kazakhs and wishing to reinforce morality and the foundations of power in the steppe, resolved to instil Islam into the Kazakh steppe. It cannot be said that Catherine the Great's attempts and those of her successors yielded any success to speak of: Islamization mainly concerned the elite. From an organizational point of view, the steppe did not see Central Asian mullahs coming from the south, but Tatar mullahs coming from the north, who soon became infected with local pagan prejudices and who were assimilated into, and dissolved among, the Kazakhs.

Life on the eve of the Revolution boiled and bubbled in the Kazakh steppe. The Kazakhs found themselves drawn into the fashionable political movements of the time, adopted from Turkey, Russia and from Europe. Some advocated a reformed and worldly Islam, others preached liberalism in its purest form, while others still, having read Karl Marx to the full, dreamed of world revolution for all oppressed peoples. Very soon the latter were able to apply their doctrine in practice; for the remaining Kazakhs this experiment came at a high price.

[10] True, the most informed historians refute this 'heroic' version of events and believe the reason for the rebellion was a banal striving to return the pasture lands that had been taken by the Russian colonial powers.

NOMADISM – THE ETERNAL RIDDLE OF THE GREAT STEPPE

For thousands of years the invasions of nomads have instilled terror into all the settled peoples. Residents of China, Central Asia, Iran, Eastern Europe and the Middle East have waited in fear for the latest attack from the Great Steppe. All the great steppe empires finally collapsed and died out, leaving scholars the still unsolved riddle of nomadism. So what contribution to the history of humankind have the nomads made? Were they just merciless destroyers or did they promote the cultural, technological and political interaction of different, remote parts of the world, and were they the creators of a unique ecological civilization, adapted to the harsh conditions of Central Eurasia?[11]

Humankind has entered the twenty-first century, yet problems linked with its ancient history continue to concern scholars and the public at large. The study of the phenomenon of nomadism is classed as one of the most interesting and, at times, painful problems. This is particularly relevant for Kazakhstan, as a significant part of its history is indeed the history of nomadic society. And this problem can be deemed painful because already by the twentieth century, nomadic societies had practically disappeared, and their destruction was accompanied by genocide, violent settlement, assimilation and loss of unique ethnic identity. All this has occurred in the history of Kazakhstan. Nevertheless, at least two main questions accompany the history of nomadism: the first concerns its ecological aspects, i.e. the interrelations of nomadic systems with nature and the creation of ideal ecological and economic relationships between people, animals and the wild, based on a nomadic system. The second question relates to the nature of interrelations between nomadic people and settled people. This aspect of history is equally painful for both civilizations.

Generally speaking, the study of nomadism as a particular historical civilization goes far beyond the research of nomadism itself and it touches a very broad group of disciplines: ethnography, archaeology, Turkology, comparative linguistics and so on; that is, it actually represents a fragment of the entire history of Central Asia.

---

[11] This is all the more odd insofar as that, while the European world has heard much of the American Indians, they knew pathetically little about their own Kazakh neighbours until only recently.

Surprising though it is, but for a considerable time there was no special study of nomadism as such; it just found itself roaming between different disciplines. For the Soviet period, such a situation is fully explicable: the study of history was forced to follow the official Marxist-Leninist doctrine and this restricted the study of the nomadic way of life to just dogmatic theory. The study of Kazakh nomadism progressed thanks to the efforts of individual enthusiasts, who could shed light on only narrow aspects, and this also continues as a parallel tradition in the West.

Certain scholars in the West placed the following theses at the basis of their concept of nomads. First of all, a specialization means a stronger dependence. This thesis is deciphered in the following way: the more specialized mobile livestock farmers are, the more they depend on the outside world. Second, nomadism is a special kind of manufacturing economy. The Kazakh steppes were one of the few regions on the planet where nomadic livestock farming could be observed in its pure form. Third, nomadic livestock farming is not fully adapted to the natural and geographic surroundings; nomads are also forced to adapt to the outside world. Finally, the nomadic economy needed resources from the agricultural and municipal world. In this way, conquering others was a means of subordinating and receiving the required products; a means brought to its logical end.

The most intriguing question in the history of the Great Steppe is the reason why the nomads were pushed to mass resettlements and to destructive marches against agricultural civilizations. Modern historiography counts a number of concepts or theories that try to explain this phenomenon. In their most generalized form they can be reduced to the following theses: various global climate changes (such as drought, or, to the opposite, excessive rainfall); the warring and greedy nature of the nomads (this point of view originates in Chinese historiography); the over-population of the steppe; the growth in production forces and the class struggle, the weakened position of the agricultural societies as a consequence of feudal compartmentalization (a classic Marxist concept); the need to replenish the extensive livestock farming economy with forays into more stable agricultural societies; the lack of desire on the part of centres of settled economies to trade with nomads; an excessive surplus of livestock produce; the personal qualities of the leaders of steppe communities; impulses towards ethnographic integration (passionarity).

It should be noted that there is an element of truth in each concept, although all of them, to one degree or another, suffer from an exaggeration of their own particular case. Modern paleographic data prove no direct link between global periods of drought or flood with a rise or fall in nomadic empires. The Marxist theory of class struggle in a nomadic society has also proved to be unfounded. The demographic factor is unclear due to the lack of sources. As for the warring nature of the nomads, the history of settled civilizations demonstrates that it was the settlers who finally created the most effective military technologies and infrastructures.

It is noted that nationality in the form of nomadic empires and other political formations developed among the nomads only in those regions where they had regular and intensive political and economic contacts with more organized agricultural and especially urban societies. This thesis is illustrated by the following dichotomy: Scythians and ancient states; Huns and the Roman Empire; Turks and China; Turks and Ancient Rus; Turks and Khorezm; Arabs, Turks and Byzantium, etc.

The nature of steppe empires was two-sided: from the outside they were reminiscent of the classical despotism of the East whose purpose was to procure additional wares from beyond the steppe, but from within the nomadic empires remained based on tribal links, without a stable tax system and a classical feudal hierarchy, implying the exploitation of the livestock farmers. The authority of the lords of the steppe was based on common law, the ability to organize military campaigns and to redistribute income from trade contributions and forays into neighbouring countries. In general, this is a rough outline of the system most applicable to the Pre-Mongolian Era.

It is considered that in their relations with settled territories the nomads used several strategies: there was the strategy of forays and plundering (Cian-bi, Turks and Mongols in relation to China; the Crimean Khanate in relation to Ukraine, Poland and the Moscow state and others); the subjection of the agricultural society and the taking of tributes from it (Scythians and Skoloti, Khazars and Slavs, the Golden Horde and Rus), and also the controlling of the trade routes (the Turks and the Great Silk Road, the Kazakhs and the trade routes joining Central Asia, China, Iran, the Caucasus and Siberia); the conquering of a settled state, the infiltration of the nomads, the creation of a new dynasty, a new ruling class and a new state with the subsequent assimilation of the nomads (the

Manchurians in China, the Mongols in China, the Khorezm in Iran, and the Kazakhs in Bukhara, etc.); the tactics of alternating forays with pillaging and the gathering of tributes, used both prior to and after conquest – by all the major nomadic formations, from the Hun in China to the Turks and Mongols in the late Middle Ages). The term 'remote exploitation' was coined in the early 1990s to explain the essence of the relations between the nomads and the people who worked the land.

It should be noted that, in the 1950s, Western scholars raised the question of the role of the early nomads. They proceeded from the fact that the advent of the European peoples should be traced back to Central Eurasia. Were the early pre-Turk nomads, in their material and spiritual culture, the forerunners of the Indo-European peoples who settled in Europe in the Bronze Age? Delving deeper into the essence of the subject, German archaeologist Karl Jettmar concluded that the civilization of the early wanderers was both unique and self-sufficient. It was the forerunner of classic nomadism, created by the Turko-Mongol nomads of Eurasia in the Common Era. A cultural foundation of sorts, from both an ethnic and a linguistic point of view, which formed the basis for both civilizations, was the so-called 'Animal Style'.

From an archaeological point of view one can only assume that nomadism emerged in the late Palaeolithic Age. Nomadism was an instinctive reaction by ancient peoples, familiar with working the land and rearing livestock, to changes in climatic conditions. This relates fully to Central Asia. A number of academics believe that, based on written sources on the Middle East, we can speak of an intensive development of nomadism at the end of 1000 BCE. The universal historical significance of nomadism is characterized by features that are both positive (expansion of the oecumene), and negative (the transition from a more productive to a less productive form of land use). The historical significance of nomadism involves the advent and development of forms of exploitation (loan of livestock) and, as a consequence, of social differentiation. However, the relationship between exploitation and dependence did not lead to antagonism. This is where we should look for the reason why the nomads could not create their own nation on the basis of a nomadic economy. Another reason is that the nomads' livestock was not exploited in the context of mass production; it was just a consumer product and a means to accumulate personal wealth.

A group of researchers approached the study of nomadism looking at the horse and pasture through history. The American academic Denis Sinor attempted to reveal a link between the rearing of horses and the economy and politics of the nomads; the creation of great cavalries and the rise and fall of the great nomad empires. Sinor believes that the staying power, modest needs and adaptability to severe climatic conditions are what distinguished the Central Asian horse and which gave it an undisputed superiority over other fighting breeds from the times of the Scythians right up to the Second World War. However, the rearing of this breed was a universal occupation throughout the entire history of Central Asia and yet only a few livestock-rearing peoples were able to create a nation of enduring significance.

Some scholars believe that to reveal what nomadic culture really is requires analysis of the ancient art of the nomadic peoples of Central Asia. The wandering people of the steppe region of Central Asia turned partially to working the land from the seventh to the ninth centuries BCE. A feature of the art of this period is the depiction of human faces as vivid mimics. The best known art of the nomadic people comes from the early Scythian-Sarmat period. At this time, the most distinguishable art form involved the use of noble metals, such as silver and bronze, on which images were made, predominantly of animals and humans. Then comes the Turko-Mongol period (fourth-fifteenth centuries), which is characterized by manuscripts and pictures at burial sites. Characteristic features of the art of the nomadic people can be highlighted over a considerable expanse, from Turkestan to Korea. It is based on the Siberian-Scythian 'animal' style, where the depiction of nature is only a supplemental element, with the image of the person or animals, in dynamic poses, tending to predominate. This art of the nomads came to have an important influence on Chinese art.

Some scholars believe that the history of the great expanses of Inner Asia (Central Asia, Siberia, Mongolia, China, Tibet and the Middle East), the Caucasus and Eastern Europe should be read in a unified context over the entire historical period, from the moment the nomadic people entered the stage of world history. The single culturological type of Central Eurasia was based on a similar type of economy and the social-hierarchical structure that came from it.

Despite the abundance of theories and concepts, modern 'nomadistics' still has many questions which remain unanswered.

The central issue in the study of the nomads, as before, is the relationship between the wandering and settled civilizations: were they antagonists or did they supplement one another in the historical process of human development?

THE HORSE IN KAZAKH HISTORY

The horse played a colossal role in the formation of the Kazakhs as a nation. Indeed, the horse played an even greater role in the history of Kazakhstan and the Kazakhs than the elephant in ancient India, sheep in early-medieval England and the camel for the Arabs.

The horse is surely the most wonderful, the wisest, most faithful and hard-working creature on the planet, accompanying humans throughout their historical development. This duet, or symbiosis if you wish, between *Homo sapiens* the wise man, and *equus*, the horse, arose at the dawn of our time and was completed very recently, in the twentieth century. It would be no exaggeration to say that without the horse there could have been no human history, at least not in its present form, and it would certainly not have made the progress it has.

Throughout history, people have used the horse as a means of transport, for food, haulage and military power, for sport, and as an item of worship and adoration. People saw horses as the fellow companions of celestial beings (the *Horses of Helios*), vested them with the divine power of inspiration (the Greek *Pegasus*) and magical flight (the Kazakh *Tulpar*), simply deified them (Alexander the Great's *Bucephalus*) and even elected them to the senate (which is what Roman Emperor Caligula did with his favourite stallion in the first century CE). Besides mythology, horses have been depicted in literature with their own inner world. Finally, for many peoples of our continent, this four-legged friend has become a part of our common folklore, which sometimes has a precise way of relaying the essence of comparison (to work like a horse), although not always deserved (to drink like a horse).

However, before becoming a part of human mythology, the horse was destined to play a great role in the establishment of human society, its economy and in the economic development of the planet. We owe much to horse meat and horse milk in medicine and dietetics. Horse meat is considered to be the best meat product for asthmatics, while *koumiss*, fermented horse milk, is reputed to be an effective treatment for tuberculosis.

It is generally believed that humans tamed the horse in about the fourth century BCE, in the Eneolithic Period. However, modern science struggles to answer the question as to when and where humans really patted the withers and fed their new animal friend with fragrant straw for the first time. However, one thing is certain: this historical world event took place somewhere in the expanses of Eurasia and, most likely, in the steppes of Central Asia

There are far stronger grounds for asserting that another historical event actually took place in Central Asia: at the turn of the second and first millennia, nomadic horsemen broke away from the herdsmen and farmers, choosing instead life with and on the horse as their main occupation and way of life. This was the second revolution after that of the Neolithic Period – nomadism broke away from agriculture and became a special form of manufacturing economy. Throughout the first millennium, the nomads of Central Asia perfected the nomadic means of production and, in parallel, they developed new geographical expanses, encroaching into settled areas. The horse for the nomad was the main mode of transport and, less frequently, the main source of food. For the peoples working the land, the horse acquired three principle functions: to be ridden, to be harnessed and to haul.

Horses had a decisive influence on three most important aspects of human activity: transport, agriculture and the military. For a considerable period of time the settled world managed without the development of horse breeding, until it had to face the superior force of the nomads, who relied almost entirely on the use of horses. The first historical encounter of the settled world with those on horseback took place in about 1700 BCE when tribes of Hyksos invaded Egypt from Asia Minor and conquered. The Hyksos, whose origin is still a mystery, brought horse breeding and harnessed transport to Egypt. The Hyksos disappeared, having dissolved among the Egyptians, while, from this moment on, and for the foreseeable future, the state on the Nile gained a military and technological advantage over its neighbours. With time, horse-breeding came to spread universally throughout the agricultural civilizations of western Asia and the entire Mediterranean.

However, every time the agricultural countries were forced to engage in battle with the Central Asian nomads, they suffered defeat after defeat. The Mediterranean states relied on their naval fleets and the strength of their land forces, predominantly infantry. Moving deep into the continent they were beaten by incomparably more mobile nomad forces. This is a fair appraisal, even in relation to those who had created the most advanced military machines of ancient times, the Greek Macedonians and the Romans. The invincible army of Alexander the Great was stopped by the Sakas on the right bank of the Syr-Daria (now the territory of Kazakhstan) in 329 BCE, while the Romans, headed by Marcus Crassus, suffered a catastrophic defeat at the hands of the Parthians in the Battle of Carrhae in 53 BCE. In both cases, the reason for the invincibility of the steppe armies can be clearly traced: complete supremacy in manoeuvrability, which gave a tactical opportunity to withdraw from battle in unfavourable conditions and return to battle at the right moment. At Carrhae the Parthians demonstrated another superiority, which the Mongols under Chinggis Khan were later to repeat over their opponents: an inaccessibility, thanks not only to a rapid horse cavalry, but also to heavy horse cavalry that was impenetrable for the infantry.

Up to the fifth century the Europeans were able to hold back the onslaught of the nomadic people from the depths of Eurasia. However, in the fifth century, the peoples known as the Huns entered history and destroyed the Roman Empire, leaving an enduring reminder of the supremacy of mounted armies over foot armies. On the whole, the long and hard historical process known as the 'Migration Period', which touched the entire history of Eurasia, could only have taken place thanks to the peoples with their horses from the Great Steppe. From the first millennium of the Common Era the nomads of Central Eurasia enter history's centre stage, at the same time playing the role of creators of great empires and cultural-technological intermediaries between remote civilizations. From the outset, the horse in this epoch is a military form of transport, the basis of military might and power, and a subject for barter and trade. Not surprisingly, the aristocracy of the settled agricultural peoples sought to acquire horses, which had become a symbol of a privileged status and military superiority.

The European feudal society saw the formation of a class of feudal horsemen, the cavalier, chevalier and the caballero, together with the heavy cavalry. The advent of the heavy horses is attributed to the Middle Ages. In time, knights disappeared, but this breed of horse remained, fulfilling heavy agricultural and industrial work until the twentieth century, when they were replaced by machines. The heavy knightly cavalry was fine in European conditions, where they were faced with poorly armed peasant infantry. However, coming up against a mounted opponent, which used the horse not as a sluggish, armoured monster, but rather as a means to acquire a strategic advantage with speed and manoeuvrability, the European armies of knights, as was to be expected, suffered defeat. This first occurred during the crusades when the knights had to fight the fast-moving Arabian cavalry. Then followed the invasion of the Mongols, after which Eurasia found itself for several centuries in the grip of the nomads' total military supremacy.

However, in the new era, the settled civilizations acquired their own military and technological advantage over the nomads. This occurred not only thanks to the development of firearms, as it was customary to believe, but to a great extent thanks to the development of horse-breeding and the creation of an effective cavalry. In this way the Spanish conquered the New World, while the Russian Empire made advances far into Central Asia. While the nomads, who were actually stagnating, bred the same breed of horse for century after century with their narrow fields of specialization, principally for pasture, transport and food, Europe witnessed an explosive increase in new breeds. In fact, in Europe, during the eighteenth and nineteenth centuries about 200 species of horse appeared. At the time of the Napoleonic wars, entire mounted armies fought each other on the fields of Europe, forces no less than those that existed during the era of the steppe empires. The largest and most catastrophic loss of horses, about half a million in total, occurred in the course of Napoleon's march on Russia in 1812.

Throughout the whole of the nineteenth century, priority in military might moved over to the possession of naval power and fire power, but the horse retained its strategic importance right up until the First World War, when, on the battlefields of Belgium and Flanders, it finally lost its significance as a strategic military resource. The horse went into battle at the soldier's side for the last time during the Second World War in 1939: the Polish Horse Cavalry bravely yet recklessly endeavoured to stop the German tanks near Warsaw; the mistake was repeated in 1941 by Soviet Marshal Budenny. Finally, the Mongolian mounted forces took part in the destruction of the Japanese Kwantung Army in Manchuria in 1945.

With technological progress and the universal spread of machines, the number of horses in the world fell steadily. By 1930, there were about 120 million horses, while in 1970 there were just a little over

60 million. Today, there are fewer than 40 million horses across the world. In the early twentieth century, Russia had the world's largest number of horses, with about 40 million grazing its fields, meadows and steppe lands. On the eve of collectivization in the USSR there were 32.6 million; after it there were 21.1 million. At the end of its existence the Soviet Union had 7–8 million horses (about 10% of the world's equine population) and this is with the USSR having the world's greatest potential for horse-herding.

In the mid-nineteenth century there were about 4 million horses in Kazakhstan (representing approximately 13% of the total head of livestock), while from the moment the country joined with Russia the number fell steadily, a result of both political and socio-economic reasons. In the second half of the nineteenth century a market mechanism came into play: the type of livestock reared by the Kazakhs was in response to heightened market demand for sheep's wool and lamb. The catastrophe that was the collectivization of 1931–32 had at its heart a purely political motivation: the numbers of horses in Kazakhstan fell to a level never seen before, namely, to about 300,000 head in all (in 1928 there were 3.5 million). The development of virgin lands, which required the requisition of an enormous amount of pasture, also put pay to a blossoming in horse-herding. And all the same, by the early 1970s thanks, they then said, to the 'committed policy of the party and the government', the number of horses was brought up to 1.2 million and, on the eve of perestroika, to 1.5 million. After a dramatic change in the economic model in the early 1990s, this number began to fall at catastrophic rates. At present, there are some 985,000 horses in Kazakhstan, although experts believe these figures are understated: as a result of privatization, a considerable part of the livestock, was taken away from state control and, accordingly, from the statistics.

So, Kazakhstan, a great steppe state, the prosperity of which was ensured for thousands of years by its herds of horses, is now experiencing a dramatic period of separation from its equine past. In order to revitalize the horse-breeding industry in Kazakhstan, faced with an ever-decreasing number of horses in the republic, perhaps it is time for a moratorium to be declared on their slaughter. The best response to this issue must come from Khan Kasym: 'We are residents of the steppe; our possessions and goods are not rare and they are not valuable. But our greatest riches are our horses.'

KAZAKHSTAN IN THE EARLY TWENTIETH CENTURY

In 1900, Kazakhstan was a territory that was set in its ways on the outside and still patriarchal in nature. On the great steppe expanses, just as hundreds and thousands of years before, the nomads grazed their livestock, moving in a century-long rhythm that remained unchanged from season to season, from north to south and from south to north. Yet this system, in existence for at least two thousand years, was experiencing intense internal changes. Major rail routes were being built through the steppe, towns grew and developed, coupled with an infrastructure, social institutions, education and healthcare, and, most importantly, trade was developing at a fast rate.

At the start of the century, Kazakhstan was controlled from three centres – Tashkent (Turkestan), Orenburg (the Steppe District) and Omsk (General Governorship of western Siberia). A decree was issued in 1900 which obligated and encouraged the settlement of the Kazakhs from the Syr-Daria Region. However, the European colonization of the steppe regions progressed at a much faster rate. In the first twenty years of the twentieth century, 17 million dessiatinas (a dessiatina being the equivalent of 2.7 acres) were given to three million Russian settlers (500,000 families). The Slavic population in these regions grew in the pre-Revolutionary period from 15% to 42%. The traditional nomadic economy of the Kazakhs, built upon the extensive pasture-based livestock rearing was eroded away and their way of life was destroyed. In the northern regions the Kazakhs quickly turned to agriculture. In the southern regions, where there were considerably fewer Russian settlers, there were also fewer settled Kazakhs. In the north-eastern regions Kazakh farms that dealt with agriculture accounted for about one half. However, the Kazakhs who could not or had no wish to change their way of life had only one thing they could do, and that was to move south. In this way, a potential for conflict accumulated in the southern regions of Kazakhstan and it was here where the most acute struggle unfolded for the possession of the irrigated lands, which were equally suitable for grazing livestock and for agriculture.

In general, the ratio of settlers to local population, as a result of the grand programme of colonization, which was implemented in three phases, from the 1860s to 1912, was 3 million Slavs to 5 million Kazakhs. The numbers of urban population also grew.

Some 40,000 people dealt in steppe trade, with a network of markets scattered all over northern Kazakhstan and southern Siberia. Thanks to British finance, Kazakhstan's mineral resources were developed and by 1916 over 18,000 Kazakhs were employed in the mining industry. And yet 90% of Kazakhs continued to remain nomads, combining, to a certain extent, livestock breeding and agriculture. The livestock numbers in the steppe grew (1885–1916) from 17 million to 30 million. At the same time there were structural changes afoot in livestock farming: there was a rise in the relative number of cattle, which required less pasture land and which were more lucrative to maintain. Changes in the Kazakhstan economy progressed in parallel with the transformation of political and social structures.

Literature in the Kazakh language, written in Arab script and, as a rule, on religious themes, became more widespread. Throughout the entire nineteenth century about 70–80,000 such books were published but, in the early twentieth century the Kazakhs saw a real explosion in publishing. Books and periodicals in the Kazakh language were printed in St Petersburg, Kazan, Ufa, Tashkent and other centres of Islam in the Russian Empire. Between 1900 and 1917 over 200 books were published and a major part of them involved publications of a social nature, the heroic epics and other models of traditional verbal creativity. The first Kazakh-language newspaper appeared in 1888; much more came after 1905 but for political reasons, none lasted very long.

The main focus of this period was the Kazakhs' switch from a tribal conscience to a national one. The world view of the Kazakhs, which previously often ended with the family group or at the perimeter of a mountain village, now reached a generally national level. By the beginning of the century four political trends had emerged in Kazakh society. The first of such trends was that of the so-called 'enlighteners'. These were the first generation of intellectuals who had encountered Russian education. They viewed the union with Russia as a positive step and they sincerely believed that the Kazakhs needed to learn Russian and adopt the European style of education. They had a critical view of Islam and they spoke out against the activity of the Tatar mullahs, while at the same time marvelling at the 'pure' and unclouded Kazakh traditions. They were the bearers of tradition, which proceeds from famous characters in Kazakh history – Chokan Valikhanov, Ibrahim (Ibrai) Altynsarin and Abai Kunanbaev. What was most important for all these people was the acknowledgement of the need to become familiar with Russian language and Russian culture as a principal condition for modernizing Kazakh society and helping it to survive.

Much less is known of another trend, which could be called the conservatives. This group of poets could be characterized by the term *Zar-Zaman*, meaning 'time of lament'. These poets were fierce antagonists of everything Russian and they idealized orthodox Islam and traditional social and moral values. Their works tell of the era of the Khans' power as being a golden age, free of corruption and the exploitation of the colonial period.

The third group are classed as the nationalists. This movement arose after contact had been made with Russian culture and education, when, in the early twentieth century, young Kazakh doctors, teachers, engineers, writers and poets no longer wished to strive towards copying European culture but concerned themselves instead with the search for their own national identity, albeit within the social, cultural and political reality of the Russian Empire. A major step in this direction was the struggle to use Islam as an element of Kazakh identity. Although the nationalists set themselves no specific objectives, the effect of this was a strengthening of the political role of Islam among the nomads. The activity of the nationalists also gave rise to two trends in the spiritual life of the Kazakhs and their renaissance. The first was a heightened interest in the family and tribal history of the Kazakhs, popularization and absolutization of genealogy, where a set, conceptualized and idealized image of the Hordes and the family-based structure dominated intellectual debate. The second trend was an interest in the Turkic heritage. In political terms the result of this was a growing liking for Turkey. Many young Kazakh intellectuals travelled to the cities of the Turkic world, as far as Istanbul, thus forming a fabric of a unified intellectual Turkic community. The representatives of this generation shared the views of the Russian liberals; they formed the Alash party, condemned or took a neutral stance on the uprising of 1916 and in 1917 formed two governments, in Orenburg and in Kokand.

The fourth movement was a rudimentary socialist group. Although in composition it was predominantly Russian, it had an influence upon the Kazakh workers in the major cities, in the mines and on the railways. From this group came a number of leaders for the future revolution that was to have such a massive impact on the entire former empire. The failed harvest of 1912 and the mass impoverishment and epidemic that followed as a result promoted significant growth in the socialist movement. From 1894 to 1906 there were sixteen Marxist groups in Kazakhstan, whose views were undoubtedly more radical than those of the representatives of the other more liberal groups. From the point of view of education the Marxist groups were, as a rule, not so well educated as the representatives of other groupings, but they always combined visits to the madrasah and the Russian school. The ideology of the Kazakh elite, which was destined to totally change the face of Kazakhstan, emerged from these latter two movements. From the merger of nationalism and communism came the phenomenon of the so-called 'Muslim National Communism', which withstood the principles of the class division of society into nations, 'those being oppressed and those who have been oppressed' and which called on the 'poor' nations to fight for their freedom from the 'rich'. This phenomenon was characteristic for all Turkic peoples of the Russian Empire.

The involvement of the Kazakhs in the political struggle on the Russian political stage between two revolutions led to an ever more active demand for Kazakhstan autonomy within the empire. The moderate wing of the intelligentsia and the elite both pursued this objective, but a large part of the Kazakh population believed that the solution to the problem was to be totally rid of the Russians and to reclaim their lands. The moment of truth came in 1916, when the government in Petrograd, through its naïve decree on the mobilization of those of different faiths into the Russian Army, which was fighting a war against the Turkish Sultan - the leader of all Muslims, gave rise to a mass uprising in central and southern Kazakhstan as well as in a large part of Turkestan. The uprising shook the very foundations of Russian rule in Central Asia and it would only be a matter of time until the region was to join the Russian Revolution of 1917. In the course of the uprising, which was accompanied by terrible violence from both sides (it was bitterest in the regions of the greatest expropriation of land from the Kazakhs for transfer to the settlers or to public funds), a split occurred within the Kazakh opposition. This was due to the fact that some of the intellectuals condemned the extreme nature of the armed battle, while others (Dzhangildin, Bokin) saw the armed battle as the only way to get rid of the hated tsarist regime. The latter were later to join the Bolsheviks, whose ultraradical ideology for a time appealed to the Kazakh nationalists, while the former were to make up the skeletal structure of the future Alash Horde.

From early 1918, the Alash Horde competed for power with isolated and poorly supported Marxists. These were still just isolated groups, united around charismatic leaders in the Syr-Daria region, where the main battles of 1916 had unfolded.

With its moderate and collaborationist policy, the government of the Alash Horde was doomed. Its flirting with Kolchak and dithering between reds and whites led to a situation where the remnants of its power and authority were lost. In 1919, the revolutionary-minded Kazakhs took centre stage in Kazakh politics; they were resolute in their support of the Socialist Revolution and the Bolshevik regime and they supported the reds in their battle with the Basmachi movement in Central Asia. A greater political intimacy became possible between the Bolsheviks and the radical Kazakh nationalists thanks to the opportunities that the new regime opened up for them: the dispossession of the Kulaks (the devastation of the Kazakh and Russian farms), and the secularization (the closing of orthodox schools) and socialization (the shift of control over nationalized property into their hands) of society as a whole. The Muslim National Communists directed their foreign policy ambitions, to use the term of the great French orientalist Alexandre Bennigsen, against Bukhara, Khiva, Iran, Afghanistan and British India, to where they dreamt of spreading the great proletarian revolution.

THE SOVIET LEGACY

The Soviet experience is the most painful and, at the same time, most important memory in modern Kazakh history. In essence, without this episode, today's independent Kazakhstan would not exist. At the same time, recollections of the imperial Soviet policy continue to echo painfully in the hearts of many Kazakh families.

The Kazakhs should be given the credit they deserve: as opposed to their more Islamized neighbours they responded with greater willingness to the slogans of the Russian communists and supported the Bolshevik Revolution. The calculation was a simple one: use the revolution to gain independence (or at least an expanded form of autonomy). Moreover, the Kazakh intellectuals actively carried the revolutionary teachings to other countries – to the colonies of the European powers in Asia, which had become objects of the Comintern's mission to spread 'world revolution'. The Kazakhs, of course, are proud of this part of their Soviet history.

However, very soon, the Kazakhs, like all the peoples of the Soviet Union, fell beneath the millstone that was Stalin's dictatorship. In the 1930s, the revolutionary intellectuals were wiped out, the achievements of the revolution in terms of autonomy were scaled down and the traditional nomadic culture was subjected to near total destruction. Recollections of this period continue to evoke a bitter taste throughout the Kazakh nation. The traditional nomadic way of life was almost completely eliminated and Kazakhstan took the path of industrialization and the extensive development of agriculture, as a major resource base for the Soviet economy. As a result there was a great influx of populations from other parts of the USSR into the republic, predominantly of Slavic origin.

In addition, Stalin conducted extraordinary and often awful experiments from time to time, involving the resettlement of populations, evidently trying to repeat fifth-century history. As a result of the Soviet dictator's experiments, Kazakhstan found itself (against its will) housing not only Russians and Ukrainians, but also many other peoples from Eurasia: Germans, Koreans, Caucasians, Dungans, Uygurs, etc. This is how the ethnic face of contemporary Kazakhstan was formed: a face that surprises, one that is a blend, beautiful and benevolent and where one can discern features of both Europe and Asia. The Kazakhs shared all they had with their guests, remembering the misfortunes and even despite these misfortunes, which they had suffered not all that long ago during the period of communist collectivization.

The mixing of the races and peoples in Kazakhstan continued even after the death of the great dictator. In the 1950s and 1960s new settlers continued to arrive in their millions, to open up the valuable lands of the 'Soviet Frontier'. The Kazakhs fought bravely and heroically on the many fronts during the Second World War and hundreds of thousands of soldiers returned to the steppe after exhausting battles, decorated for the taking of Warsaw, Budapest, Vienna, Prague and Berlin. They returned with surprise to see how their ancient land was being rapidly modernized: mines and factories, plants and highways, railways and pipelines were springing up everywhere. The modern European world, the total self-destruction of which they had just witnessed in Europe, had suddenly appeared in Kazakhstan.

But there was more. Moscow chose Kazakhstan to implement its strategic projects in the creation of missiles and nuclear weapons, ventures into space and the testing of the very latest strategic weaponry. Kazakhstan came to house the nuclear test site at Semipalatinsk, the Baikonur space station, missile bases and strategic bomber commands. In the 1970s, Kazakhstan thus became an important element in the strategic might of the Soviet Union in its confrontation with the West. The Soviet leader Leonid Brezhnev, under whom the USSR reached the peak of its powers and became a superpower on a par with America, was much indebted to Kazakhstan, where he had worked in the 1950s. In the future, Brezhnev retained his affection for Kazakhstan, demanding that it supplied ever more meat and grain to Russia and provided more and more land for strategic purposes.

A figure like Leonid Brezhnev is worthy of special digression. Brezhnev's work in Kazakhstan had several consequences. First, there were the political consequences: through party and political lines he supported his friend Dinmukhamed Kunaev,[12] who also became a symbolic figure for Kazakhstan, an icon for an entire era, just as Brezhnev was for the entire Soviet Union. Second, there were economic consequences: Brezhnev devoted particular attention to ensure Kazakhstan always received its share of subsidies and followed the path to transformation into an agrarian and industrial republic. Third, Brezhnev was fond of the Kazakhstan capital and did much to turn Alma-Ata into one of the most beautiful cities in the Soviet Union.

Today, only the older generation recalls that in the mid-1950s the future general secretary once lived in a small green house in the centre of the city. Those from Alma-Ata and Kazakhstan who encountered Brezhnev recall that he remained a jolly optimist and a responsive comrade, one who loved a good joke and a party. Evidently, Brezhnev was reluctant to leave Kazakhstan. The wicked tongues asserted that he left behind not only decent comrades, but a host of delightful swarthy girlfriends as well.

His friendship with Dimash, as he liked to call Dinmukhamed Kunaev, stood the test of time and the test of political intrigues. As

---

[12] Dinmukhamed Kunaev came from a engineering and academic background. For over twenty years he governed Kazakhstan (from 1964 to 1986) and made a significant contribution to the development of the national elite.

soon as he came to power, Brezhnev supported the return of Kunaev to the post of first secretary of the republic and the removal of the previous secretary, a protégé of Krushchev, who had supported separatist projects related to the creation of an Uygur autonomy within Kazakhstan and the appropriation of Virgin Lands into Russian territory. He later brought Kunaev into the Politburo of the Central Committee of the Communist Party, the supreme political authority in the USSR, which significantly enhanced Kazakhstan's status within the Soviet hierarchy, placing it third after Ukraine, while, in a strategic military sense it could even have been classed as the second most important republic of the Union. In his turn Kunaev repaid Brezhnev with loyalty and friendship. After the death of the general secretary, the Kazakhstan leader tried to continue Brezhnev's line in the Politburo and to support his people in the power struggle, which he paid for in 1986, when he was ousted.

Brezhnev travelled many times to Kazakhstan and to his beloved Alma-Ata. However, now his seat as leader of the republic was occupied by his friend Dinmukhamed Kunaev, combining the features of a leading academic and cunning political fox, a committed communist and secret nationalist. Understanding the need to bow to Moscow, which was still capable of suppressing any sign of discontent among the union's republics with an iron fist, Kunaev elected to follow a strategy of the gradual 'Kazakhization' of Kazakhstan. In fact, this involved the creation of a national Kazakh elite, which could take the fate of the nation into its own hands at the right moment.

When Gorbachev commenced his ill-fated perestroika, an unsuccessful attempt to reform what was an already non-viable Soviet economic and political system, the first thing he did was to try and reinforce Moscow's power in Central Asia and other parts of the Soviet Union. In 1986, the Soviet centre's removal of Kunaev from office resulted in a student revolt, which demonstrated to the world that the days of the Soviet empire were numbered. And, indeed, there was something symbolic in the fact that five years after Soviet troops had crushed the students' uprising, in December 1991, an agreement was signed in Alma-Ata, which brought to an end the history of the USSR - the greatest geopolitical and socio-economic phenomenon of the twentieth century.

The Soviet Union was no more and, in 1992, Kazakhstan entered unknown territory, which the US President Bill Clinton was later to call 'the Brave New World'.[13] Not for the first time in its history, Kazakhstan was setting out on a road, both exciting and dangerous, to build a new country.

HOW TO CREATE KAZAKHSTAN: A LITTLE GEOPOLITICS AND ECONOMICS

To say that Kazakhstan after the fall of the Soviet Union was in a difficult position is to say almost nothing at all. The situation for the republic was extraordinarily difficult in every sense, with its geography, geopolitical climate, demographics, history, economics and politics all presenting unique problems and dilemmas.

Independent Kazakhstan had at its disposal an enormous territory, with borders of a colossal length and with little protection (with the exception of the Chinese direction), with a small population and a poorly-developed transport and communications system. Kazakhstan's economy was totally structured to meet the demands of the Soviet system with entire regions of the country tied into the external market and not to that of the republic. There was almost nothing connecting these regions apart from an administrative attachment to the same country. Indeed, the regions of Kazakhstan had become seriously isolated in terms of economic structure, the nature of production, as well as demographic and national composition.

One of the most complex problems inherited by Kazakhstan from the pre-Revolutionary and Soviet eras and which is rigidly tied in with external issues was the ethnic problem. The ethnic composition of Kazakhstan was distinguished by a clearly-defined dichotomy: Kazakh-Russian, Turkic-Slav, Muslim-European and so on. Built into this system were various corporate, group-based and social interests, which by no means promoted national unity in the young Kazakhstan nation in the process of its formation.

The main external issue was expressed primarily in the fact that the overwhelming part of the so-called Russian-speaking population was accustomed to living not in Kazakhstan but in the USSR. Their interests, life experiences and moods were oriented towards the Soviet way of life. Therefore, it was natural that after the fall of the empire their sympathies shifted automatically to Russia. The

[13] Coined from the novel of the same name by Aldous Huxley

German population voted with their feet: the first half of the 1990s saw mass emigration of the Germans of Kazakhstan to Germany, which had a considerable downward impact on the economy. In the mid-1990s the outflow of the Russian and Russian-speaking population reached its peak. Against this background a swift change to the demographic balance in the republic became evident and Kazakhstan came to acquire the features of a Kazakh state.

From the first days of its independence, and even prior to the official fall of the USSR, Kazakhstan, like it or not, found itself dragged into a grand geopolitical game. It concentrated all the problems of the post-Soviet period: the fall of a superpower and Russia's weakness, which played into the hands of the West; the problems of the nuclear heritage; the Caspian Knot; the onset of Islamist fundamentalism from the south; the shadow of China, which had risen sharply over the East; the persistent striving of the West, of the United States in the first instance, to impose its rules of the game, and much, much more.

It still seems improbable how, in these most complex of conditions, the leadership in Kazakhstan managed to find the right way through the various, and generally contradictory pressures coming from all directions. What resulted came to be known as the 'multi-vectored policy'. A kind of 'black hole' appeared in the region following the departure of Russia, a so-called geopolitical vacuum, which many powers rushed to fill. The leadership in Kazakhstan observed with some surprise how Moscow was letting a strategic and economic infrastructure that had taken so much effort to create simply fall to pieces.

Moscow treated its former Union republic partners as tiresome spongers. This was particularly evident in the history of the rouble zone, from which Kazakhstan and other republics were simply pushed out. Fortunately, there were no serious consequences from this error. What is more, Kazakhstan and Russia were able to unravel the other problems they faced: the fate of the Baikonur space station, the Soviet debts, the delimitation of the Caspian Sea and so on. However, as a result of Moscow's short-sighted policy in the early 1990s, Russia's departure came to acquire an irreversible nature.

In the early 1990s, Central Asia came face to face with the world of Islam, which considered the region as part of it. The events of the end of the 1990s and the early 2000s confirmed the foresight of those who had warned of the threat of militant Islamism for

Central Asia immediately following the fall of the USSR. This is a world of many faces and each of the Muslim players was pursuing its own policy. The greatest activity in the early stages came from Turkey, although its strategy in Central Asia bore no relation to Islam, rather it was founded on an illusory concept of Turkic unity. With time this concept proved to be a failure; the countries in the region rejected the new 'elder brother' Ankara, which was being imposed upon them by the West. Nevertheless, Kazakhstan succeeded in directing the development of links with Turkey to purely trade and economic ends, to the mutual benefit of both parties.

The greatest concerns in relation to the export of militant Islam to Central Asia existed in connection with Iran. However, in the second half of the 1990s Iran joined the anti-Taliban coalition with Russia, India and countries of Central Asia. The real threat from militant fundamentalism was of an indirect nature and came from Pakistan and Saudi Arabia. In its relations with the World of Islam, Kazakhstan had to decide many unknowns. It was necessary to show the Islamic countries that Kazakhstan was 'one of them', while at the same time not frightening off Russia and the West with its excessive intimacy with the Muslim world. Naturally, Kazakhstan was not flirting with the Islamic world, seen by the West as alien and dangerous, without good cause. At the same time, Kazakhstan was searching and feeling out new opportunities on the international stage to reinforce its own security.

Kazakhstan's relations with China deserve special attention. This is an instance where the leadership of the young and independent state had to break the stereotypes in relation to its neighbour; stereotypes that had been imposed from outside and those of its own. Concerns were unwittingly aroused by the colossal demographic parameters of this country and its direct vicinity to Central Asia. In short, a certain psychological barrier had to be overcome in order to become closer to the People's Republic of China. It is to Beijing's credit that as regards its geopolitical ambitions relative to Central Asia, it structured its policy in such a way so as to almost totally disperse the concerns harboured by the post-Soviet states and the West. For a long time Russia believed that there were no reasons to be wary of China, that it could not take its place as the patron of the region. The West, on the contrary, proceeded on the basis that China could have a favourable economic influence on the region. In the early 1990s, neither

Russia nor the West could have anticipated that China would dare to claim the role of a fully-fledged geopolitical player in the region.

Using gentle diplomatic pressure with a latent demonstration of its might, Beijing was able to 'convince' its partners in negotiation of the need to acknowledge the problem of the 'disputed' territories and then to agree that the 'disputed' territories belong by right to the Celestial Empire. It should be said that China managed to sweeten the pill and shroud the ceding of territory with a programme of intense economic cooperation, and even with the formation of a broad political organization – the Shanghai Five (later the SCO). In this way Kazakhstan was able to improve its relations with its huge neighbour. As far as the geopolitical ambitions of Beijing were concerned, it carefully masked them, thus gradually dispersing almost all doubts. Furthermore, after the events of 2001–2002, the impression was formed that China was consciously withdrawing from involvement in any geopolitical games in their traditional sense.

The history of how the USA came to Central Asia and consolidated its position is a part of that great geopolitical game that the American strategists have been playing some fifty years now, under the influence of their own theoretical and geopolitical designs, and which they just cannot get round to finishing. The complex diplomatic and political game that began for Kazakhstan with Washington back in 1991, still continues to this day. Bringing the Soviet Union to collapse, the United States believed that they had a 'legal' right to handle its legacy as they saw fit. Falling under the most important geopolitical legacy was the great expanse of the Caspian Basin and Central Asia, control over which would establish a dominant position in all of central Eurasia. It was these considerations that formed the basis of Washington's strategy in the region and its focus was directed towards Kazakhstan, the most important and most valuable geopolitical element of the former USSR.

Kazakhstan did have the means for political manoeuvring in its relations with the USA, in the form of the Soviet nuclear weaponry held on Kazakh soil and which the USA was very keen to be rid of. And so Chevron came to the Caspian, followed by other Western and transnational companies. These events had serious geopolitical consequences; if at first Washington saw the Caspian project as dead in the water, economically speaking, it soon saw the broad geopolitical opportunities to be gained from control over Caspian oil.

The USA kept a close eye on the nature of the relationship of the Central Asian states with Russia and Iran to ensure that it did not get to a point where they could fall under the influence of Moscow and Tehran. As noted above, the West initially looked kindly on the activity shown by China. Furthermore, the USA was trying not to permit a strengthening of fundamentalism, of whatever form and to prevent the region becoming a source of proliferation of weapons of mass destruction or their materials and technologies.

In this way, the international and domestic policies of Kazakhstan in the first decade after it acquired independence were formed in strictly predetermined conditions. Today it can be asserted that the Kazakhstan leadership, of course, had a choice. However, this was often a choice of the lesser of two evils; between the bad and the very bad. In the geopolitical, economic and political chaos of the early 1990s the logic of survival and the striving to preserve stability pushed Kazakhstan to create a behavioural model which would help it to emerge unscathed from the difficult situations into which it had been driven by geopolitics and the contradictory interests of the big players.

With time, Kazakhstan's leaders came to master the skills of diplomacy and foreign policy. Kazakhstan was generally successful in finding common ground with different powers and, more or less, it kept itself on a par, even in the face of an obvious inequality in political power. Of course, if Kazakhstan's diplomacy was backed up by serious economic potential, an effective army, large population, etc., the Kazakh foreign policy and its debut on the geopolitical chessboard would have been more effective. Nevertheless, Kazakhstan could produce politicians from its ranks, who could guide the ship of state on a stable course through the storms and reefs of world politics.

As with other nationalities in Soviet society, Kazakhs had a hierarchy made up primarily on the basis of professional and corporate solidarity. The ancestral remnants of the Kazakhs should be sought in such customs as respect for one's elders and an affinity with like-minded people. The consequences of the collapse of the previous socio-economic system and the introduction of market conditions came in two forms. First, a killer blow was dealt to the privileges and social status afforded to the previous Soviet elite; the intelligentsia and its structures (the academic institutes and universities) were literally laid to waste. Second, however, another process followed immediately afterwards, and even in parallel: the elite set about teaching its children in the new, prestigious spheres, linked with the market economy, management and finance. In this way, the principles of stable traditions and the reproduction of the elite were preserved in their principal features. On the whole, the Kazakh elite had to fulfil the same objective it faced in Soviet times, under a state-controlled economy, but under new conditions: to retain control over resources. And in this it was successful.

In Soviet times the Kazakh elite had to bow to Moscow and this restricted its ability to control economic resources. However, Western sociology states that, in addition to the so-called economic capital, there is also the 'cultural capital' and the 'symbolic' capital, which are understood to mean the acquisition of knowledge, specific skills, the accumulation of prestige and respect. Once Moscow's control had gone, the Kazakh elite made full use of the cultural and symbolic capital they had at their disposal.

The ruling trend of the early 1990s, one of ethnic unity, made way for the fragmentation of Kazakh society. One thing that divides Kazakhs is the relationship to the Russian and Kazakh languages, as an attribute of ethnic belonging and social status. A sign of this trend is the striving of the Kazakh elite to preserve their children's knowledge of Russian and to educate them in Russian-speaking schools. However, this trend occurs against a background of a more extensive process, that of the upbringing of an internationally-oriented (i.e. pro-Western) generation in the new Kazakh elite. And it is this element of the elite, no longer exclusively Russian-oriented, yet also not purely Kazakh in upbringing, who will have to play the decisive role in the future Kazakhstan.

The explosive events of the late 1990s and early 2000s proved a major test of security, statehood and independence in foreign policy. While market reforms were being implemented a generation of young entrepreneurs had grown up. Gaining financial resources, they came to hanker after power. As a result of this new opposition[14] receiving moral and political support from outside, the stability of

---

[14] The 'new' opposition is the name given to the opponents of official authority, which emerged and got rich in the course of the reforms, in contrast to the 'old' opposition – the supporters of the communists and of socialism in the Soviet style.

the Kazakhstan society was seen to be under threat. And yet Kazakhstan is now acknowledged by Washington and Brussels as the most stable and dynamically-developing country in Central Asia. President Nazarbaev's difficult and initially unpopular reforms of the previous decade have appeared to produce results and the population is now living under a more liberal climate, with a lesser dependence on the state.

Nursultan Nazarbaev, Kazakhstan's leader and first president, enjoys immense popularity, despite the fact of alleged voting irregularities and Parliament voting for him to remain in power for an unlimited number of terms. He is seen as popular both in the West and in the East, among Kazakhs and Russians who live in Kazakhstan. He is a welcome guest in Moscow and throughout the CIS, where he is seen as a main proponent of close integration of the post-Soviet states.

HOW TO SURVIVE IN THE MODERN WORLD: KAZAKH DIPLOMACY

Continuing and supplementing the previous section, let us now consider other ways in which Kazakhstan has survived in the modern world - specifically in the context of diplomacy. Kazakhstan officially uses the term 'multi-vectored diplomacy', which was first introduced in the mid 1990s. In fact, concealed beneath the term 'multi-vectored' was a balancing of the different geopolitical centres of power that had exerted an influence on Kazakhstan and on Central Asia as a whole.

The multi-vectored approach to foreign policy first came into play in the early 1990s, a time remembered well by the populace. Kazakhstan received its independence at the end of 1991, coupled with a whole host of problems: a thousand or more Soviet nuclear warheads, a huge territory to keep secure and a diverse, polyethnic population, one half of which still did not feel itself to be citizens of a sovereign Kazakhstan. This was in addition to having two enormous neighbours, extensive, unprotected borders and unresolved frontier issues, incredibly rich natural resources, coveted by neighbours near and far, and a remoteness from the sea and communications with the world.

As soon as Kazakhstan had obtained independence, a multitude of advisers poured forth, both desired and undesired. There were those who taught us how to build democracy and a market economy, others – how to protect human rights. Still others called on us to return to our historical, cultural and ethnic roots and, finally, there were those who wanted to persuade us not to break the Soviet economic and political umbilical cord. Accordingly, each party, with their own vested interest, depending upon its geopolitical and international weight, tried to apply pressure on Kazakhstan.

The country's first test of flexibility was with the issue of the Soviet nuclear legacy. As luck and the geopolitical status would have it, the republic found itself in the same team with Russia, Belarus and Ukraine, all inheritors of the Soviet nuclear arsenal. But it was upon Kazakhstan that the greatest pressure was brought to bear. The West suddenly came to suspect a liking for the Islamic world and a striving to assist in the creation of a so-called 'Islamic nuclear bomb' for certain Islamic countries. This all proceeded against a bloody conflict that had unfolded in Tajikistan on regional and confessional grounds. In order not to miscalculate and to bargain coherently with Washington on the nuclear issue, Alma-Ata needed clear advice from Moscow, but it did not get any. Left very much to its own devices, therefore, the Kazakhstan leadership set about a cautious game, either declaring itself to be a 'temporary nuclear state' or agreeing to the unconditional removal of missiles. As a result, Washington was simply unable to work out what they were really to expect from Kazakhstan. It seemed that Moscow understood what was going on, but in response to the puzzled questions of the Americans, they only shrugged their shoulders helplessly.

Soon a new and very important element entered the picture- Caspian oil, and Kazakhstan exercised the principle of nuclear weapons in exchange for investment to good effect. We should remember that at the time Washington still had no idea of the true scale of the reserves that had been discovered and predicted in the Caspian Sea and, also, it was wary of Russia's reaction, without knowing how weak Yeltsin's regime actually was. In these conditions, the administration of George Bush Snr tried not to take risks, but in exchange for Kazakhstan's agreement to remove ballistic missiles from its territory, it applied pressure on Chevron and encouraged it to come with investment into what was then perceived to be not a particularly lucrative Caspian enterprise. It was only later that the Caspian was to become a pivotal element in American geopolitics in Eurasia.

Relations between China and the Soviet Union had started to improve even in Gorbachev's time. After the fall of the union, the separate republics had to deal with the Asian giant individually. However, even back in the time of perestroika, Beijing had clearly set Moscow a condition: total normalization of relations would be possible only if the frontier question was resolved, along with the problem of the so-called disputed territories. Incidentally, these territories were 'disputed' only in China's eyes. With a vested interest in economic cooperation with the People's Republic and also proceeding from completely logical considerations that it was better not to have problems with such a neighbour, Kazakhstan was also forced to agree to acknowledge the sovereignty of China over the desert wastelands, which, during the era of Soviet-Chinese confrontation, actually belonged to no one. However, from a social and psychological point of view, the very fact of the transfer of territories was a painful thing for our public opinion.

The well-known aphorism that it is harder to be a friend of America than to be its enemy is fully applicable to Kazakhstan and its complex, to say the least, relations with the USA. In 1994, the presidents of Kazakhstan and the USA signed a Charter on strategic partnership. And while the charter imposed no obligations on the USA, Kazakhstan, as was soon revealed, had to strictly observe the spirit and the word of the agreement, namely to build democracy and a market economy, observe human rights, run honest elections under international monitoring and all this under the watchful eye of the 'strategic partner', America.

It was revealed that the White House was seriously intent on intervening in Kazakhstan's internal affairs. Nevertheless, Astana was able to get away with a course for Kazakhstan, which was more or less independent, especially in matters of an internal nature, the strengthening of the twin pillars of power and statehood. The reasons, as always, lay in Washington's geopolitical obsession; its striving, at any cost, to implement its Caspian strategy.

The Caspian direction of foreign policy proved to be the most complex and the most multi-vectored aspect in all of Kazakhstan's foreign policy. On the one hand ever-growing pressure was to be felt from the principal investor, the USA, and also from the 'brotherly' Turkey, while on the other hand a difficult dialogue had to be maintained with the closest ally, Russia and other post-Soviet states, including such an ambiguous partner as the leader of Turkmenistan, the now-deceased Turkmenbashi and also Iran, which put forward business-like and, at first, apparently reasonable proposals. A firm *Yes* could not be given to one side for fear of offending the other. A categorical *No* was not an option, either, to protect the national interests and even the security of Kazakhstan.

In such conditions Kazakh diplomacy displayed the utmost resourcefulness and balancing skills. For a considerable time Astana kept completely silent about the Baku-Tbilisi-Ceyhan pipeline and used this time to intensify negotiations on the legal status and regulation of disputed matters with Russia, the principal partner on the Caspian Sea. At the same time, Kazakhstan came out with wholly non-binding statements about the acceptability of the Iranian route, which was sure to appease Tehran. In 1998, Kazakhstan and Russia achieved a breakthrough in delimiting their sections of the Caspian Shelf, which heralded the start of a genuine process of the delimitation of the sea and the resources found beneath it. It is true that Iran was removed from the equation, but this became more a problem for Azerbaijan and Turkmenistan, which Moscow and Astana gave the opportunity to sort out with Tehran themselves.

Moreover, after reaching agreement with Russia, Kazakhstan found its hands were not tied in terms of the Baku-Tbilisi-Ceyhan project. Kazakh diplomacy could now speak out on the subject of this pipeline with relative freedom. The meaning behind the statements made by the Kazakh side, and which it continues to make, comes down to the following: build what you like; we are prepared to pump our oil over any pipeline and even over all of them at once, as long as there are buyers and as long as oil prices do not fall. It is probable that Russia did not like this position much. To complete the picture, Kazakhstan managed to bring two more players into the Caspian game. The first was China, with which a ten-billion dollar agreement was signed and which was christened from the start as 'the project of the century'. However, with Beijing, Kazakhstan encountered a partner that was at least as, if not more, skilled in the diplomatic and 'multi-vectored' game.

The southern, or Islamic direction, always remained among the most complicated in Kazakh diplomacy. In its relations with the Islamic world, Kazakhstan, for a time and in the interests of progress, had to discard its European image and, depending upon the specific situation, don a turban, fez or dhoti. Put simply, Kazakhstan did not stop those who wanted to see it as a close Turkic relative, a part of the Islamic world and at times as a true heir of

Soviet-Indian friendship. Following this path and adhering to specific political and economic objectives, Kazakhstan enabled itself to become involved in various, previously 'exotic' international associations: the ECO (Economic Cooperation Organization), ICO (Islamic Conference Organization) and the union of Turkophone states, headed by Turkey.

To be fair, it should be pointed out that the flirting with Ankara, waving the flag of pan-Turkism, Turkic unity and acknowledging Turkey as a new, 'elder brother', soon ended. It was replaced by a real and intense, mutually beneficial, economic collaboration. However, in Turkish high society, Kazakhstan also saw another channel in its relations with the West and with NATO. The matter was more complex with Iran and Pakistan; Islamic states in spirit and in form. Relations with Pakistan and India required that a distinct parity be observed in the number of visits and agreements signed and in the volume of diplomatic activity conducted.

There is another aspect of foreign policy which should not be overlooked and, not surprisingly, it relates to the integration of the post-Soviet space. From the earliest days of the advent of the Commonwealth of Independent States (CIS), Kazakhstan made truly titanic efforts to achieve integration. Indeed, like no other republic of the former Soviet Union, Kazakhstan was keen to retain traditional links, not least in the context of its dependence on the union-wide economy. Furthermore, there was also the question of securing joint strategic security. Despite the fact that such an objective was not altogether welcomed by its friends in the West, Kazakhstan persisted in proposing more and more new integration initiatives.[15]

And all the same, the multi-vectored policy did bring wholly tangible results. Kazakhstan was able to make full use of the advantages it had been bestowed by history and by geology and it endeavoured to minimize the risks and threats that had arisen from its not altogether successful geopolitical and geographical position, becoming a leader in economic reforms and economic development

[15] The boldest of these was the offer to create a Eurasian union in place of the CIS, voiced by the President of Kazakhstan at Moscow State University in the Spring of 1994.

among the countries of Central Asia and even the CIS. In so doing, Kazakhstan retained good relations with all the players in the grand political game and with its neighbours and countries further afield that were important to it. Problems of security were also resolved by entering or cooperating with various associations, blocs and unions, including the Collective Security Treaty Organization (CSTO), the Shanghai Cooperation Organization (SCO) and the NATO Partnership for Peace.

It is specific people who form policies, including foreign policy. It is obvious that our foreign policy direction was formed and directed by the country's senior leadership, yet a major role in the successful implementation of the multi-vectored foreign policy course was played by managers who easily found common ground both with the West and with the East. Kazakhstan was very fortunate in that the foreign policy authority and other structures, responsible for national security, were peopled by a generation of specialists, Eurasian in spirit and patriotically-minded, who were enthusiasts for their cause, accepted an open view of the world and, most importantly, were loyal to the interests of their country.

KAZAKHSTAN AND ITS NEIGHBOURS: WHO THINKS WHAT OF WHOM

The old saying goes, 'If you want to know who you are, ask what your neighbour thinks.' Wording it differently you could say that if you want to know who you are, compare yourself with your neighbours. The time has now come when it would be opportune for the Kazakhs to adopt both versions of the saying.

For centuries, the Kazakhs' neighbours and their ancestors saw these people as ruthless nomads, who from nowhere atop their wild horses had crashed down upon them – peaceful farming folk and townspeople. The Chinese were of the same opinion and they tried to keep out the nomadic world with their Great Wall. The Russians, likewise, had experienced the full delights of political control of the nomadic horde, which remained in the national memory as a 'yoke'. There are some sharp-witted scholars in California who call the nomad's conquest and enslavement of the settled countries, along with the collection of tributes, a 'remote exploitation'.

More or less the same opinion of the nomads was held by their Muslim neighbours of Khorezm, Persia, India and the Arab peoples of the Middle East.[16] However, historical memory is a tenacious thing; it turns to stone and transforms recollections into stereotypes. This is how the settled neighbours have retained a stereotype from the time of the Middle Ages that the Kazakhs are a warring people and, therefore, dangerous nomads. Human psychology tends to assign the most negative features to all that is alien and hostile: wild, ignorant, pagan, living in unsanitary conditions, smelling of goat's milk, etc.

As the settled civilizations progressed, their ruling classes came to see the nomads as 'backward barbarians'. This became characteristic for the Russians, who, in the New Age managed to gain command over the eastern territories of the Golden Horde, to which it had once had to bow before as slaves. The Russians saw the Kazakhs as nomads, frozen in a time gone by, who had forgotten the military glory of their great ancestors. The Russians saw themselves, starting from the reforms of Peter the Great, as unequivocally European.

This would have been funny if it had not been so sad: the residents of the agricultural oases of Turkestan, speaking in tongues similar to that of the Kazakhs and confessing the same religion, Sunni Islam, also tried to look upon their immediate neighbours as poor relations from the past and, accordingly, they regarded them with a feeling of superiority. Thus, they devised jokes with the main character being a steppe-Kazakh, who is terribly afraid upon first hearing the loud call of the muezzin to prayer in the big city.

Credit should be given to the Kazakhs where it is due: they, too, made up countless witty jokes and funny stories about their neighbours, who behaved in their natural environment like little children. The Kazakhs found much to mock in the mercenary, small-minded nature of their neighbours and what they saw as their slave-like psychology. The principal difference lay elsewhere: the Kazakhs had managed to preserve their reigning aristocracy, which was highly revered in the East.

---

[16] As regards the Arabs, we should remember that they, too, not long before this, were also 'ruthless nomads' in relation to the peoples they conquered in the course of the creation of the Caliphate. If we go further into analogies, we should remember that this role was fulfilled by all peoples when they entered history's centre stage, be it the Teutons, the Slavs or others.

After Kazakhstan had been joined first to Tsarist and then to Soviet Russia, when the Kazakhs displayed a fine sense of adaptation to changing conditions and culturalization, they again became the butt of jokes for their more traditional neighbours - for example, for trying hard not to be separated from Islam as well as for other aspects of their medieval way of life. At this time the Kazakhs were laughed at and accused of excessive Russification, although in reality there was only talk of modernization. To be fair, it should be said that to one degree or another, modernization concerned all peoples of Central Asia, but it was only the Kazakhs who were able to turn it into a real tool to build a bridge to the future.

This became clear several years after independence was achieved. While Kazakhstan was confidently conducting economic reforms and the Kazakh elite was effectively investing its incredibly rich human potential (spearheaded by a young generation of market-oriented, Western-thinking individuals), into the post-Soviet market modernization, its neighbours were concentrating on a return to their historical roots. In practice, this meant the revival of archaic public institutions, together with the Islamization and degradation of the education system.

This divide between the Kazakhs and their neighbours was very apparent at the start of the new century, when no one would think of laughing at or looking down on the descendants of the ungovernable nomads. On the contrary, hundreds of thousands of the descendants of the proud bearers of the 'ancient Islamic civilization' rushed to Kazakhstan in search of work, to find markets for their fruit and, generally, for a better life. They quickly became an integral part of the local economy, occupying its least prestigious niches. Similar processes were witnessed in Russia, too.

Credit should be given to the Kazakhs, who, rather than making a habit of humiliating or laughing at the new *Gastarbeiters*, even though they used them for their own benefit, wisely prepared for the time when their neighbours would begin to find a way out of the economic hole into which they had been led by arrogance and poor management on the part of their own governments. This confirms once again the truth that the tolerance and flexibility acquired by the Kazakhs over the course of their history leads to wisdom, as long as the lessons of history are correctly perceived. However, sometimes the price can be too high. No one knows the price of this truth better than the Kazakhs.

With time the Kazakh elite taught their Russian and Western partners to speak with them as equals. The greatest puzzle today, and the greatest challenge for them are the Chinese, with whom economic and political necessity dictate business should be done. However, the Kazakhs have not forgotten their Eastern origins, so the chances are really very high that the Kazakhs will not allow their dialogue with the Chinese to become a monologue.

In so doing, without flattering themselves over their current successes or drawing comparisons with that famous character from the La Fontaine fable who could be bought with flattery, the Kazakhs always remember how their neighbours treated them in the past. They are diplomatically silent as to their opinion of them, remembering the past but thinking about the future.

FAR FROM HOME: KAZAKHS ABROAD

Meeting our compatriots abroad no longer generates surprise. After the fall of the Iron Curtain, many Kazakhs and Kazakhstanis work, study, do business and simply travel all over the world. However, there are times when we encounter Kazakhs with a different past. They do not speak Russian and their Kazakh tongue has a strong Turkish accent. At times they have exotic passports, from such countries as the People's Republic of China (i.e. Kuomintang, or Taiwanese), Saudi Arabia or Pakistan. These are the Kazakhs whom history has flung to the distant corners of the world and further, yet they still see themselves as Kazakhs.

We know that the most significant Kazakh diasporas are found in China, Mongolia and Turkey (except the post-Soviet space – Russia, Uzbekistan, etc., where more than two million Kazakhs are concentrated). Kazakhs may also be encountered in India, Afghanistan and Iran, in Arab countries and in Western Europe – in France, Germany and Sweden. Their appearance in these places, far from Kazakhstan, is a consequence of the dramatic historical events which shook Central Eurasia from the eighteenth to the twentieth centuries. The history of the resettlement and movement of the Kazakh clan families from their native steppes is worthy of comparison with the biblical Exodus.

The appearance of Kazakhs within what is now Xinjiang dates back to the early 1760s. We imagine what this time was like: only recently had the cruel battles with the Jungars calmed down, the Small Horde had already accepted citizenship of the Russian

Empire and Ablai-Khan was manoeuvring between Russia and Qing China, trying to preserve the Kazakh state. By this time the Qing had finally disposed of the remnants of the western Mongols (Kalmyks and Jungar Oirats), weakened by long wars with the Kazakhs for domination in Central Asia. The final strike on the remnants of the Jungars, who had forced their way from the Caspian-Volga region back to their native Tarbagatay mountains, came in the form of savage epidemics. Following this and utilizing the fact that the Jungars were dying out, the Manchus set about their indiscriminate slaughter. As a result of this genocide by the Manchu powers, the pastures of the Iliisk district were almost completely cleared and, after 1761, Kazakh tribes began to occupy them without prior arrangement (predominantly representatives of the Kerei and Naiman tribes).

This movement towards Eastern Turkestan was not arranged politically: the migratory mountain villages, or auls, having emerged from under the jurisdiction of Ablai-Khan and the local Chinese authorities had come to see them as citizens of the Qing Empire. After Ablai's death in 1781 they were finally fixed with the status of Chinese subjects. From this time on the Kazakh population became an important element in the ethnic, economic and political history of Xinjiang. However, it should be pointed out that for an entire century the Kazakhs moved freely from Xinjiang to the Kazakh steppes, knowing no boundaries between empires and often even totally unsuspecting of their presence. There was a new influx of the Kazakh population into western China after the crushing of the uprising of Kenesary Khan in 1847. A border was finally established between the Russian and Chinese empires in 1883, under the Tarbagatay Protocol.

The main reason for resettling Kazakhs into areas controlled by China was the political and economic instability in the Kazakh steppe. We recall that the latter part of the nineteenth and early twentieth centuries saw a period of active Russian colonization of the steppe. The next mass influx of Kazakhs into Xinjiang occurred in 1916 after the crushing of a vast uprising, encompassing all of Russian Turkestan. This event saw the movement of about 300,000 Kazakhs. However, this episode had no impact on the demographics of the region: in 1918 almost all Kazakhs were returned by the admnistration of republican China.

The next major wave of refugees was not long in coming: in addition to the huge number of victims among the nomadic population, the collectivization in Kazakhstan brought about another wave of resettlement: tens and hundreds of thousands of our fellow tribesmen fled the USSR for China from 1928 to 1937. Entire mountain villages (or auls) of Kazakhs went not only to western China, but also to the south, through Turkmenia to Iran and Afghanistan and to the Far East. According to eye-witness reports, some of the auls even got as far as the Pacific Ocean, travelling across the whole of Siberia.

As opposed to the Kazakh population in Soviet Kazakhstan, the Kazakh refugees did not simply try to preserve, they actually fought for the right to maintain their previous, traditional way of life. By the mid-twentieth century a cultural and linguistic gulf had arisen between the Kazakhstani Kazakhs and their fellow tribesmen abroad. The Kazakhs in China saw themselves as Kazakhs, just as before: free-roaming nomads and Muslims. They tried to live as their ancestors had lived for centuries, and they distanced themselves mostly from the Chinese and also often enough from the local Uygur population. Yet the political storms that had raged in China in the first half of the twentieth century were sure to have drawn the Kazakhs into the battle for the self-determination of Eastern Turkestan.

There were two attempts to create an independent state in the region: first, in 1933, the Islamic Republic of Eastern-Turkestan was proclaimed in Kashgar, which the military governor Sheng Shicai dealt with in the same year, using detachments made up of Russian migrants and with the support of the USSR. The Kazakhs took part in an anti-China uprising and chose Sultan Sharip as their leader. The repressions on the part of the Chinese led to the Kazakhs moving deeper to the east and north-east.

In 1943, there was an uprising among the Altai Kazakhs. The insurgents were given refuge and military support from Mongolia, which had been controlled by the USSR. The following year, the rebellion spilled over into the Ili District and in November 1944 it was again proclaimed the Eastern Turkestan Republic (ETR). The main reason for the Kazakh's active involvement in the rebellion against Chinese rule was the same as in Soviet Central Asia: the attempts by the authorities to enforce a sedentary life on the nomads, disarm them and force them to live by the rules of settled peoples. The Kazakh detachments became the principal military force of the ETR, in which the major political power belonged to the Uygurs.

In the course of the rebellion, from among the military leaders came forward the fearless and charismatic Osman Batyr, who was soon celebrated as a symbol of the liberation movement; a kind of Kazakh Robin Hood. Osman Batyr fought the Chinese from 1939 to 1950 and in this period of over ten years his name became shrouded in legend and fables, turning him, especially after his death, into a figure of epic proportions, comparable with heroes such as Koblandy Batyr or Kambar Batyr. The ever-changing military and political situation forced Osman Batyr to either fight with the Uygurs against the Chinese, or against the Uygurs, the Russians, the Mongols, etc. However, the main objective for Osman Batyr and his army was to ensure independence for the Kazakhs, their freedom and a nomadic way of life away from the infringement of any outside force.

It was a cause that was doomed to fail. From 1945, the Soviet Union openly turned away from the Kuomintang and came to support the Chinese Communist Party. As a result, Osman Batyr fought his last battles against the communist forces of the PLAC. Osman Batyr also ended his life as hero and legend, just as he had fought: he was captured when trying to save his daughter, but his horse slipped on the ice of Lake Gaz Kul. The hero was executed in Urumchi as 'a bandit and robber' but, to his last seconds, Osman Batyr remained proud, with the virtue of his epic ancestors.

The Muslim minorities in Xinjiang continued their resistance up until 1954, but the remains of Osman Batyr's army made their choice; in 1951 about 15,000 people crossed Tibet into India. This was not the first time the Kazakhs had crossed the immense mountains of Tibet and the Himalayas, yet the route of Osman-Batyr's army could not have been more dramatic.

It covered over 4,000 km, during which, in search of freedom, the Kazakhs overcame the lifeless Lobnor and Taklimakan deserts and the world's highest mountains of the Himalayas in Tibet. The journey, during which the Kazakhs fought enemies, the cold and their hunger, lasted two years. All their livestock and the majority of those undertaking the epic March were lost on the way, leaving only 350 emaciated people to finally reach India. This passage undoubtedly had a resonance across the world. In February 1955, a member of the British Parliament, Godfrey Lias, published a description of these events in the *Times* (later, Lias was to write a book about the Kazakhs, which he actually called *The Kazak Exodus*). In the summer of 1953, astonished residents of the Indian part of Kashmir watched the arrival from the mountains of ragged and emaciated men and women (practically all the children had perished). They were what was left of Osman Batyr's Kazakh army. Negotiations to decide their fate lasted almost a month (the Indian authorities had no wish to accept another section of the Muslin population into the already restless Kashmir and damage relations with China and the USSR). However, in the end it was British tolerance that won the day when Jawaharlal Nehru personally gave permission for the Kazakhs to reside in the Indian Republic.

The Indian climate was to have a catastrophic effect on the natives of Central Asia and hundreds of Kazakh refugees died during the rainy season. Pakistan, too, attended to the fate of the Kazakhs. The last of the Kazakhs left Srinagar in 1969. Some of them, following the example of their relations, the Uygurs, chose to go to Saudi Arabia. Yet it was in their kindred Turkey where the Kazakhs found their second homeland, where many Kazakh migrants from Iran, Afghanistan and Indostan found true shelter. Of course, such a policy was set in the Turkish strategy to support 'Outside Turks' (the official name of the Turkic people beyond the confines of Anatolia). Together with the Uzbeks and the Uygurs, the Kazakhs were considered under official Ankara policy as 'Turkestanis'. Some of the Kazakhs were settled in Turkey's mountainous regions, where the geographical conditions were suited to their customary nomadic way of life.

In time, the Kazakh emigrants mastered their own field in the processing industry: tanning, which became their calling card in Turkey and Western Europe. In 1961, the new Turkish constitution permitted migration from the country and the Kazakhs made full use of this right and the agreements on migrant employment, signed by Ankara with West Germany, Austria, the Netherlands, France, Switzerland, Sweden and Australia, had a part to play in this. As a result, with rights of Turkish Gastarbeiters, the Kazakhs gained the right to live and work in these countries. Preference in migration went to Cologne and (West) Berlin, to where Kazakhs often migrated directly from the nostalgically named Altai-Koi region in Turkey. And today the most united and well-organized Kazakh diasporas are found in these cities.

In the early 1980s, Kazakhs could be found across Western Europe, Australia and the USA. A major reason for this was the military coup in Turkey and the general deterioration of the employment market. Thus, the descendants of Osman Batyr, who to his very death had fought for the Kazakh nomadic identity, gradually transformed into peaceful peasants, honest craftsmen and skilled tradesmen; a kind of irony of fate and a sign of the times.

While historical storms were raging over the Kazakhs in the USSR and China, the Mongol Kazakhs could live in relative peace and quiet. In socialist Mongolia our fellow tribesmen were able to live and develop in stable economic and political conditions. What is more, the totalitarian regime and Moscow gave a certain preference to the Kazakhs when recruiting party and administrative personnel, as they constituted a kind of counterbalance to Mongolian nationalism.

The Mongolian Kazakhs were the only ethnic minority in this country to have at their disposal a sufficient administrative and cultural autonomy. For Ulan Bator the Kazakhs also played the role of a buffer between the Khalkha Mongols and the Oirats (the western Mongols), extinguishing the secessionist mood of the latter. The privatization that began in the 1990s worsened the economic status of the Kazakh farmsteads. This process coincided with the halt in Soviet economic assistance and the collapse of the entire previous economic infrastructure of socialist Mongolia. In the early 1990s, these Kazakhs began to return to Kazakhstan, believing that they would discover their true motherland. The reasons for the migration of the Mongolian Kazakhs lay in the downfall of the socialist system, in the accompanying change in the previous political and economic relations in the former People's Republic of Mongolia and the wave of privatization that then followed.

Mongolian Kazakhs are mainly associated with the phenomenon of the current internal social life of Kazakhstan, with the Oralman, the ethnic Kazakh who has returned to his or her ethnic homeland from elsewhere in the Central Asian region. The greater mass of migrants from Mongolia was comprised of urbanized Kazakhs who, having lost their jobs in the towns and cities, preferred to leave for Kazakhstan than return to the rural localities in western Mongolia.

The intellectuals and students settled in Alma-Ata. The resettlement of the Mongolian Kazakhs in the fertile southern regions of the republic was blocked both by administrative measures and by the objective situation on the market. The settlers found it hard to find their feet in the homeland of their ancestors and some of them decided to return to Mongolia. The Mongolian government supported the Kazakh migration, but then it also welcomed their return to Mongolia, proceeding from concerns of Oirat separatism and from economic considerations, as the Aimak territorial units of western Mongolia had simply been deserted.

From the mid-1990s the government of Kazakhstan has been conducting a wide-ranging policy on the return of the Oralmans to the homeland of their ancestors. In addition to Kazakhs from Mongolia, fellow tribesmen come here from Iran, Afghanistan, Uzbekistan and Turkmenistan. This process is incredibly complicated from social, cultural and linguistic points of view. Kazakhstan today is a government that is European-orientated in its development, with a considerable part of its population preferring to speak Russian. The process of adaptation is slow and is accompanied by specific problems.

This process cannot influence the principal strategic vector in the development of the Kazakhs, both within Kazakhstan itself and the Kazakh diasporas. This vector involves the unavoidable rejection of the traditional nomadic heritage and the move to a contemporary, modernized way of life. Tellingly, this process has not only touched the life of the Kazakhstani Kazakhs, for whom it was to a great extent a forced choice, but also of the descendants of the Chinese Kazakhs who settled in Turkey and countries of the West, for whom the choice was purely voluntary.

IN SUMMARY: HOW KAZAKHSTAN CAME TO BE

To understand modern Kazakhstan and to answer the question as to how this unusual and fascinating country came to be, we should look at its geography and its history. Kazakhstan is the world's ninth largest country and the second largest state of the CIS after Russia. It is also one of the richest in terms of its natural resources and it is seen as the most stable of all the post-Soviet states. The territory that was traditionally seen as 'Kazakh lands' and where the Kazakhs performed their seasonal nomadic cycle was somewhat larger than the Kazakhstan of today. It stretched from the banks of the Volga and the Caspian Sea in the west to the Tarym and Ili rivers in the east, from Siberia in the north to the Syr-Daria River in the south. This region covers an area of about three million square kilometres.

From about the end of the eighteenth or the early nineteenth centuries and until the Russian Revolution of 1917 Kazakhstan was a part of the Russian Empire. From 1790 to 1916 the Kazakhs organized many rebellions and uprisings, and they staged a national war of liberation against the Tsarist colonial administration. The main consequence of the Kazakhs' contacts with the Russians was their influence on the region's economy. The frontier fortifications soon turned into centres for trade and economic growth. The strategic railway from Orenburg to Tashkent crossed the Kazakh steppe and gave rise to active Russian colonization, breaking down the traditional nomadic society.

In 1920, Kazakhstan became a Soviet republic, a part of the USSR. Soviet rule became a kind of experiment in the creation of a modern Kazakh identity. The central Soviet government made significant efforts to transform traditional Kazakh society so as to incorporate it more quickly into the Soviet system. From the 1920s, Soviet power began attacks on Islam. The tragedy of collectivization and forced settlement led to a radical breakdown of the Kazakh culture in the 1930s. And then the Soviet regime started industralizing Kazakhstan, a process that continued throughout the Second World War and especially into the 1950s and 1960s. By this time, Kazakhstan had turned into a major industrial republic for the USSR. The second important event saw the development of the so-called Virgin Lands in the 1950s, to increase grain production. A major consequence of this campaign was the mass Russian and European colonization of the Kazakh steppes.

From the 1960s up to the 1980s Kazakhstan strengthened its position as a key republic and a major centre for raw material production for power generation, a major grain and meat producer, a home for the Soviet Union's considerable nuclear arsenal and the place where its space programme was implemented. At this time, the ruling Kazakh elite started to exert active control over the economic and political life of the republic and support a cultural renaissance.

The summit held in Kazakhstan's capital Alma-Ata on 20–21 December 1991 officially heralded the end of the Soviet Union and the formation of the Commonwealth of Independent States (CIS). A little before this Kazakhstan had proclaimed its independence, which took place on 16 December 1991. The socio-economic and political system that formed thereafter in Kazakhstan cannot be considered outside the full context of international relations that existed at the moment the Soviet system fell. The forming of modern-day Kazakhstan, with its financial, economic and political system, with all its pros and cons, its foreign economic strategy, investment, regional, social and tax policies, etc. – all this was to a great extent determined by two powerful factors: the external environment and the political will of the country's leadership.

After the fall of the USSR, Kazakhstan found it had at its disposal an enormous territory with extensive and unprotected borders, with a small population and a poorly-developed transport and communications system. The economy of Soviet Kazakhstan was entirely designed for existence under the Soviet system of division of labour. Whole regions were tied more to the external market than to that of the republic. There was almost nothing connecting these regions apart from an administrative attachment to the same country. The regions of Kazakhstan had become seriously isolated in terms of economic structure, the nature of production, and demographic and national composition.

One of the most complex problems inherited by Kazakhstan from the pre-Revolutionary and Soviet eras and which is rigidly tied to the external factor was the ethnic problem. As we well know, the ethnic composition of Kazakhstan was distinguished by a clearly-defined dichotomy: Kazakh-Russian, Turkic-Slav, Muslim-European and so on. Built into this system were various corporate, group-based and social interests, which by no means promoted national unity in the young Kazakhstan nation in the process of its formation.

It is customary to call Kazakhstan's diplomacy a 'multi-vectored policy'. This was a forced and, to a great extent, intuitive decision, to draw a balance of relations with partners that, in terms of political and economic power, were superior to Kazakhstan in many areas, using the contradictions and interests of one against the other. The Kazakhstan leadership drew on such a mechanism of relations with Russia, which enabled Kazakhstan on the one hand to retain full sovereignty, and on the other to retain the ability to manoeuvre on the international stage in the complex geopolitical battle that had commenced over Central Asia.

In its relations with the Islamic world Kazakhstan was faced with the need to address many unknowns. The Islamic countries had to be shown that Kazakhstan was 'one of them', as it were, while not getting on the wrong side of Russia and the West by pursuing too close a relationship with the Muslim world. The principle objective involved ensuring the country did not have to deal with any unexpected surprises, linked with the activities of the militant Islamists, who were gaining in strength on all fronts. At the same time

Kazakhstan was searching and feeling its way on the international stage for new opportunities to enhance its own security.

Consequently, Kazakhstan has had to deal with a major challenge as a result of 'restrictions' coming from various sides. Kazakhstan's new partners began to promote a specific dialogue, in which their perception of the young state varies according to their own cultural, economic and political requirements.

With time, Kazakhstan's leaders came to master the skills of diplomacy and foreign policy. As a rule, Kazakhstan was successful in finding common ground with different powers and, more or less, it kept itself on a par, even in the face of an obvious inequality in political power. Kazakhstan could produce politicians from its ranks, who could guide the ship of state through the storms and reefs of world politics. A major test of our security, sovereignty and independence in foreign policy came with the challenging events of the early 2000s, which led to a new geopolitical situation in the region.

The internal development of Kazakhstan in the period of its independence was no less dramatic. There are wide-ranging and acute discussions in Kazakhstan society about the place and role of traditional culture and the nature of Kazakhstan's modern identity. In today's Kazakhstan, nomadism is no longer a vibrant tradition among the Kazakhs, although it continues to retain its place as a fundamental element of the national consciousness. It is connected with art and poetry, rituals and language; it is a link between the Kazakh people and surrounding nature. Nevertheless, traditionalism is still alive among the Kazakhs and other ethnic groups of the country, despite the Westernization and modernization that is taking place.

Traditional Kazakh society was characterized as a mixture of dependence and independence, subordination and insubordination. Its traditional hierarchy was constantly undermined by the everyday need of the nomadic way of life to make decisions in its own right. Thus, despite the outwardly very strict framework for mutual kinship, loyalty and subordination, each nomadic community, for purely objective reasons, continued to remain an independent economic entity with its own economy and potential to choose its own location for itself. Such flexibility added a certain dynamism to the tribal structure during the periods of constant change within the intra-regional balance of political forces. This elasticity was lost after Kazakhstan was annexed and after the enforced settlement, at which point the tribal structure lost its real functional significance and retained only a genealogical status.

Many experts believe that the Soviet heritage is the foundation-stone of the modern-day Kazakh identity. The changes that occurred in Kazakh society during the Soviet era represent the chasm that divides the Kazakhs in Kazakhstan from their brethren in China, Mongolia and other countries.

2

Population and Culture

A FEW PARTING WORDS TO THE TOURIST RISKING A VISIT TO THIS COUNTRY

So, you have decided to visit Kazakhstan and you know next to nothing about it. You have been encouraged to give it a go by an indomitable striving towards the unusual and extraordinary; or perhaps distant recollections from books you read in your childhood have pulled at the strings in your soul. Possibly this idea has come to you after you have tired of your measured and comfortable life in the big city; perhaps you cannot bear the company of your relatives, friends or co-workers. Whatever the reason, on your own account, you have finally found a travel agent who has offered you a trip to the unknown and the exotic that is Kazakhstan.

Perhaps, and this is something we do not rule out, your gaze simply fell upon the map and, in the expanse between the enormous countries of Russia and China you noticed another country; a country unknown and suspiciously ending in -stan, reminiscent of a place where bearded Islamists hunt Western tourists. Another option not to be excluded from the list of possibilities is that you could not find the right agency and you have simply purchased a plane ticket off the cuff, just to find out what this unexplored place called Kazakhstan is really like.

Whatever your motives for coming to Kazakhstan, you will be both disappointed and charmed. Disappointed, because you will encounter a completely contemporary level of service of the highest Western standards. You could live here for several weeks without ever seeing anything resembling *The Thousand and One Nights* and you will not see the primeval nomads in the spirit of Chinggis Khan and Timur. Instead, you will be pampered in five-star hotels, such as the Regent Intercontinental, which are no different from the kind you will find in New York, London and Paris. You can travel around in the very latest Mercedes and BMW models and even fail to realize you are in the centre of Asia. There is no shortage of large and dull museums, sterile restaurants and cold galleries, styled in the very latest designs.

And yet there is much more to find in this country. You can climb mountains with their peaks in the clouds or gaze into the deep abyss of canyons that cut through the great Kazakh steppe. You can ride the fastest horses in the world and lose your head with the clean air of the steppe winds in your face. You can see sunrises and sunsets to make you quote Zoroaster, born of this earth, in saying that in this country the sun is born and dies every single day!

You may march in the sands that once stopped the invincible soldiers of Alexander the Great. You will see Buddha, turned to rock, transformed by his divine power into an eternal image of divine goodness, gazing with a gentle smile upon the peaceful flow of the great River Ili. The banks of the river are home to copses, once the hunting ground of dinosaurs. Break a stalk of feather grass in the steppe and smell it; you will sense the genuine fragrance of history, feel the heavy tread of the millions of horses and armies of the great conquerors of the past.

All of this and more is what Kazakhstan is about; a wonderful interweaving, a synthesis of geography and history. Yet the most important thing in Kazakhstan is not its nature nor its past alone. It is its people. Here you can find sincere and genuine friends, if your heart is open to them. If you are lonely or heartbroken, you are sure to find comfort and oblivion.

So that this short book does not come across as a blinkered advertisement for one country, we would like to add that in Kazakhstan there are the usual unpleasantries that can be encountered anywhere in the world. For example, your luggage may be lost as in Amsterdam, nimble pickpockets may lighten your pockets as in Rome, or you may be the victim of a con trick just as in London. Kazakhstan does not have the number of beggars as in Mumbai, New Delhi or Islamabad, but that is not to say you will not find them.

To conclude, it could be said that before setting off to Kazakhstan you would do well to stock up on a sense of humour, which will never go amiss, plenty of patience, just in case, and, most importantly, a good dose of optimism. All this will help you to understand better and even come to love many things, customs and mores you never knew before and which you may encounter for the first time in Kazakhstan. If you are visiting Kazakhstan but not for the first time, assist the inexperienced traveller with some helpful advice; you will be rewarded in heaven in due time.

So, off you go! Today's Kazakhstan awaits.

HOW TO TELL WHO YOUR COMPANION IS

When in Kazakhstan you will be conversing a lot of the time with the local residents, in which case you will be faced with two important tasks. The first involves guessing who is standing in front of you at that particular moment. The second is not to let your companion know that you have guessed.

The point here concerns ethnic origin. On the whole, this is a delicate subject and it is not customary to speak openly about it, just as it is not customary in any other decent society. However, it is important for you to know who is standing before you, first, in order to avoid displaying a lack of tact (for example, offering pork to a Muslim, although this is a separate matter in its own right) and, second, to understand the place your companion occupies in the local hierarchy and, therefore, what his or her capabilities are.

As already mentioned, the ethnic picture of modern-day Kazakhstan is incredibly varied, thanks to the whims of history and the social experiments of Comrade Stalin. Here, the most diverse peoples of Eurasia live next to one another, when they lived from time immemorial at opposite ends of this great continent. Germans and Koreans are a perfect example.

On the whole it is customary to divide the population of Kazakhstan into two main groups: the 'Europeans' (Russians and other Slavs, Germans, etc.) and the 'Asians' (primarily all the Turkic peoples – the Kazakhs, Uzbeks, Uygurs and so on). Such a division probably goes back to the pre-Revolutionary period. Sometimes Koreans (who in due course adopted Christianity) and Dungans (Chinese converts to Islam) are classed in the Asiatic group, which is explained by their external appearance alone. However, the division into 'Europeans' and 'Asians' in this way remains very much a provisional matter, as among the 'Asians' there are many who look like genuine Europeans. Many anthropologists believe that Russians are 'Europeans', but then only at a stretch.

Several use the term 'Muslim' without applying any religious significance at all, only wishing to stress that the subject relates to the Turkic peoples. This is convenient for identification of the Tatars, who are incredibly close to the Kazakhs in the sense of language and culture, but more similar to Russians in their external appearance.

This should be important for foreigners as they often commit the common error (and not only in Kazakhstan-in all the post-Soviet countries as well). To your question as to what a person's nationality is, someone who grew up in the Soviet Union will answer honestly: I am a Kazakh (Russian, Ukrainian, etc.), with their ethnic origin in mind, but at the same time they remain a citizen of Kazakhstan (without being a Kazakh), Russia (without being a Russian), Uzbekistan (without being an Uzbek), etc.

Foreign embassies in Alma-Ata found themselves in an amusing situation when they hired staff for lesser official positions from among the local population,[1] where the main requirements was citizenship of Kazakhstan. However, applicants that sat the test, the majority of whom were Slavs, answered the question in the form truthfully, stating, 'I am Russian'. Naturally, they were shown the door. It was only with time that the diplomats understood that they were turning down regular citizens of Kazakhstan, who would not have dreamed of answering the question of their nationality with the word *Kazakh*, as they had grown up (being citizens of the USSR) in total confidence that they were Russians.

The biggest puzzle is how to sort out the question of who the Kazakhs themselves are. Let us assume you have been fortunate and you have understood that the person standing before you is a representative of the so-called 'title nation'.[2] So what is it that makes a Kazakh? Southerner or northerner? Urban or rural dweller? If the person is pointedly hospitable, even obtrusive to a point, somewhat boastful and enjoys showing off, you can be sure you are dealing with a 'southerner' who in Kazakhstan are deservedly known as 'Texans'. Just like the natives from the genuine Texas in America,

[1] It appears that the Germans use the term 'Hilfskraefte' to describe this category of employee. The story originated at the German Embassy, but there were similar cases in other missions, too.

[2] The people who gave their name to their republic appeared under this odd name in the Soviet hierarchy. In Kazakhstan, the title nation is the Kazakhs; in Kyrgyzia it is the Kyrgyz people and so on. However, this does not relate to Russians in Russia, although the title nations in the Russian autonomous regions have no qualms about using this term.

this category of Kazakhs likes to exaggerate and is full of pride for the recognition of their own significance.

Moving on, let us assume that with a wonderful knowledge of Russian (or a European language) you have guessed that the person before you is a Kazakh who has grown up in the city. You can consider yourself fortunate; from this moment on communication will progress much more easily. You can comfortably touch on any subject, be it international politics, culture, rock music, or life in London or Paris and you can be sure of a good conversation. However, try to steer clear of the domestic politics of this country and its recent history, linked with the fall of the Soviet Union. It is most likely that you would be met with a stony silence.

The holiest of the holies for all Kazakhs and hidden from outsiders by a heavy veil of silence is their ancestral and tribal belonging. They conceal it from their fellow citizens of non-Kazakh origin and particularly from foreigners, although for many it is an open secret. At best you will be told a popular joke about the representatives of another, competing clan, but little more than that. This subject is seen as extremely delicate, as certain Western analysts are sure that the political process in Kazakhstan depends greatly upon the tribal belonging of one or other member of the political elite. Some of the more competent experts believe that this is altogether a myth and that origin has absolutely no impact on career growth.

If you know a thing or two about history and oriental studies, you can easily touch on this subject in an historical context. Then, if the atmosphere surrounding the conversation allows, you can move unnoticed to the here and now. But remember, you have to tread very carefully.

And a few words in conclusion. People's names (onomastics) play a major role in identifying your partners. Names of a clearly Arabic and Persian origin indicate that you are dealing with a representative of the eastern nationalities. Here it is worth remembering that the Kazakhs, in addition to names of a clearly Arabic and Persian origin, often use purely Turkic names, the origin of which you will be unable to guess if you are not versed in the local specifics and languages.

If your companion in conversation is typically Asiatic in appearance but with a European name, you can be almost one hundred per cent sure you are dealing with an ethnic Korean. However, among representatives of the older generation of Kazakhs, born in the stormy era of the 1920s to 1940s and raised in children's homes or among Russians, European names are widespread. Russians are easy to recognize, being similar to their European neighbours (although with a noticeably adapted mentality compared with that of Russians in Russia, as the Asiatic Russians themselves assert and, naturally, to their own benefit). Distinguishing Ukrainians, Belarusians and other Slavic people from among them without outside help is something you will be unable to do. Sometimes the surname is the key although, as such, this is not that important.

The fact is that, together, the representatives of the European and Slavic population constitute a large segment of society in Kazakhstan which, in the last years of the Soviet Union, was known as the 'Russian-speaking population'. A feature of this population is a common mentality, a blurring of internal differences, a striving to protect its 'Soviet' identity and internationalism in the old spirit. Nevertheless, the 'Russian speakers' are Kazakhstani patriots. They are now actively teaching their children the Kazakh language and trying to become integrated in the building of the new, post-Soviet Kazakhstan. The growth of Russian nationalism in Russia worries them and, generally, they do what they can to distance themselves from Russians in Siberia and Russia, underlining their Central Asian mentality. [3]

Today, the representatives of the Russian-speaking community are actively involved in building the new, post-Soviet Kazakhstan. Many send their children to Kazakh schools. The concept of 'Kazakhstani' has real substance. The status and position of Jews is a separate matter. There are many Jews in Kazakhstan, despite the mass emigration in the early 1990s. On the whole this group, while being specific in nature, is still a segment of the Russian-speaking urban population, while their mentality is close to that of related groups in other parts of the CIS.

National and ethnic tolerance is a government policy in Kazakhstan. The threat of ethnic-based destabilization was too high in the early 1990s. All citizens are equal, regardless of their nationality and origin. Russian is an official language, alongside the 'state'

[3] Unfortunately, there have been grounds for this. After the collapse of the USSR in the 1990s many Russians in Central Asia and Kazakhstan returned to their 'historical homeland', Siberia and Russia. They were not seen as Russians, they were envied; their property was destroyed and homes and cars set on fire. As a result, many of them returned to Kazakhstan.

Kazakh language. The government suppresses all attempts at ethnic-based division and encourages dialogue in any way it can between nationalities and religions, to which end special organizations and assemblies have been created.

So, you have guessed who the person you are talking to is; but it would be best if you tactfully make them understand that you consider them to be a Kazakhstani.

THE HOLIEST OF HOLIES: THE CULT OF FOOD

The climatic and living conditions for the Kazakhs' ancestors and other peoples of Central Eurasia were harsh. Therefore, it became synonymous with the residents of these vast steppe expanses to take care over their food, which became more than just a simple source of nutrition, but an important element of social life.

Like the nomads, the Kazakhs know their meat like no one else and it can be boldly asserted that they are champions in this field. Several years ago there was a very popular joke on the subject. The UN conducted research into 'who consumes the most meat'. The list produced put the Kazakhs in second place. The Kazakhs were furious and demanded to know who had dared to overtake them at the top of the tree! The answer was simple – the wolves consumed more. This joke just goes to show how proud the Kazakhs are of their meat culture.

The traditional staple Kazakh diet is comprised of three main types of meat: lamb, beef and horse meat. Occasionally, some regions, principally in the south, consume camel meat, although even the Kazakhs themselves now deem this exotic. In coastal regions, by the Caspian Sea and the Aral Sea (when it still existed[4]) and by the Volga and Ural rivers, the diet also included noble fish such as the sturgeon and beluga, which are by no means inferior to meat in calorie content. Furthermore, the Kazakhs continue to enjoy game in their diet, particularly the roe-deer and Saiga antelope.

Despite the regional differences, the cuisine of all Kazakhs is more or less the same. To be honest, the traditional Kazakh table for

---

[4] The Aral Sea is an example of one of the worst ecological disasters in history. This major expanse of water disappeared in the 1970s and 1980s based on a combination of anthropogenic and natural factors. However, Kazakhstan has now managed to recover the Northern part of the lake; fish have appeared there again, although the scale of the fishing industry is incomparable with that of the 1950s.

a special occasion comes down to the main and the only dish, known as *beshbarmak* or meat Kazakh-style.[5] It is difficult to describe but put simply, it is a dish piled high with different kinds of boiled meat. The dish has been modified over time; the Kazakhs have come to add dough, onion, potato and other vegetables, proving that the Kazakhs have not been a force for conservatism over the course of their history and, as they made contact with the agricultural peoples, they turned away from their monopoly on meat. However, there are the sticklers for tradition who grumble at there being too many vegetables in the beshbarmak.

Beshbarmak consists of several types of meat, but its piquancy is given by dried horse meat. Here would be a good place to digress and sing the praises of this meat. For many Europeans, horse meat continues to be something exotic, although the French have long (seemingly since their retreat from Moscow in 1812) valued the taste and nutritional qualities of this meat and they import it from Kazakhstan as a delicacy. There are even some of the Kazakhs' neighbours from among the Turkic peoples who consider it barbaric to eat horse, the faithful friend and comrade in arms.[6] However, the Kazakhs, who themselves, of course, value the horse as the best friend of the nomad, have produced a special breed of horse, reared specially for food but not used for transport purposes.

For those who have been able to value its qualities, horse meat is a fabulous delicacy. This meat is fully assimilated and, in dried form, it can last for several months, improving in taste and becoming pleasantly aromatic with time. Unfortunately, there are fewer and fewer recipes for preparing horse meat in use and it is now more and more difficult to find a properly made horse-meat sausage or *kazy*. At the bazaar you will be offered a substitute under the same name, which will most likely be poorly prepared.

Lamb or, more specifically one part of it – the head, is also an important element of the table for a special occasion. If you have

---

[5] In translation from Kazakh (*beshbarmak*) the name means 'five fingers'. This is a subtle hint that the dish should be eaten with the hands. This is the case with practically everything else; forks only appeared in the steppe in the twentieth century.

[6] This prejudice is especially prevalent among the Turkmens, who possess an incredibly rare breed of Akhaltekin racehorse. However, being nomads, the Turkmens wander predominantly in the deserts and they do not have the capability of breeding horses for gastronomic purposes.

occasion to find yourself seated at a Kazakh table you may be shocked to be seated in the place of honour and served the sheep's head to cut as the respected guest. Many Europeans are initially frightened by the sight of a boiled sheep's head with its teeth knocked out, so it is advisable to put one's prejudices aside and value the delicacy on offer. Before boiling, the head is scorched on the fire, giving the skin a particular and, it should be said, very interesting flavour.

Cutting and dressing the head is a special ritual. Each person at the table must be given a piece of the head, where each element has a particular significance and requires a certain wish. If someone is given the tongue it means you wish them eloquence. The ears and eyes are usually given to children and teenagers, wishing them good hearing and vision, in both the direct and indirect sense of the word. The brains are also served. Do not be offended if they are offered to you, thinking it is a sign that you do not have enough of your own. This is not a wish, rather a statement of fact: you are considered a truly intelligent person. You may have read of similar instances in the books of James Fenimore Cooper and Karl May about the North American Indians.

If you have been unable to overcome your aversion, ingrained by the civilization in which you live, you will be laughed at behind your back, but you will be understood. Another test is the sour horse milk, known as *koumiss*. It should be noted that Kazakh cuisine is not all meat-based, but meat- and dairy-based. Fermented milk products played an enormous role in the life of the nomad, being not only a beverage, but a food throughout the course of the day. A derivative is horse milk, which is specially treated and fermented. Koumiss is a wonderful supplement to the abundant meat dishes, which it helps to successfully digest. Indeed, it plays the same role as dry wines for the French and Italians. Incidentally, Koumiss is an intoxicating drink and can be quite strong. The foreigner at first finds it difficult to get used to this sour and, at first, sharp-tasting beverage, but with time many come to value it for its merits, especially in the heat of summer; koumiss is a wonderful way to quench the thirst. We know many foreigners who have acquired the taste and, upon their return to Kazakhstan, make a point of heading straight for the bazaar to taste the mare's milk once again.

There is also a beverage from camel's milk, known as *shubat*. It has a milder flavour, is not as sour as koumiss and it is thicker and fattier. The older generation tends to prefer shubat, but both koumiss and shubat are great ways to help digest a meat dinner.

However, we should warn that caution should be exercised when partaking of koumiss. For a weak stomach, koumiss could be disastrous and you can be sure of an upset stomach. There are even many Kazakhs who have long since moved to the cities who at times find it diffcult to to get used to the specific effect of koumiss, preferring to enjoy it at a distance. As with horse meat, koumiss has medicinal properties. For more than a decade now there has been a farm in Western Germany where horses are reared expressly for the production of koumiss which is also used in the preparation of a dozen or so creams and cosmetics. The founder of this business is the son of a German burgher, whom a cruel military fate landed in Kazakhstan as a prisoner of war during the Second World War. This German fell ill whilst in captivity with the latter stages of tuberculosis. He was saved from inevitable death by koumiss, which the compassionate natives fed to the sufferer. Returning to his native Hannover, the healed man swore he would devote the rest of his life to promoting and producing horse milk. His son continued and expanded his father's dream and the business is now flourishing. Another, similar farm can be found in eastern Germany, not far from Berlin.

There is probably no other place in the world other than Kazakhstan and Germany where you can try koumiss. Other nomadic people, neighbours to the Kazakhs (Bashkirs, Mongols and Kalmyks) also use horse's milk but in taste their beverage is clearly inferior to Kazakh koumiss. The reason probably lies in the steppe grass. Even in Kazakhstan itself, koumiss often varies depending upon the region and the season. The best koumiss is considered to be that which is prepared from the milk of fillies that graze on alpine meadows and which are milked in May and June. This means that you should try it in Alma-Ata, the country's southern capital. Spring and early summer is the best time of the year to do that.

But the cuisine in Kazakhstan is not all meat, meat and more meat. To think that is to be badly mistaken. The ethnic diversity of Kazakhstan has had a most wonderful impact on the culinary life of this most varied and mixed republic of the former Soviet Union. It is here that the culinary traditions of all peoples of the empire, Russian, Uzbek, Tatar, Uygur, Ukrainian, Dungan, Korean and European, all came together and intertwined. Turkish and Arabic fast food found its way here in the last years of Soviet rule. After independence, Kazakhstani cuisine was supplemented with exotic Chinese, Japanese and Thai dishes. The only cuisine that Kazakhstan does not have is American, but they say that such a thing does not really exist in any case. At least McDonald's has yet to open up in this country. True, some restaurants prepare excellent Mexican fahitas and burritos.

The Kazakhs have applied a creative approach to the dishes they have adopted from their neighbours. They have filled the Uzbek *plov* rice dish, Dungan *lagman* soup, Tatar *belyashi* dough pies and Uygur *manti* dumplings with meat content and incorporated them into their own diet. In simple terms, where neighbours gave preference to herbs and vegetables over meat for economical reasons, the Kazakhs were unstinting and added the amount of meat to which they were accustomed. This is why the Kazakhs have long since seen the principal dishes of their Central Asian neighbours as their own. There are even many Russian dishes, such as *pelmeni* dumplings and *blinis*, and Ukrainian *borsch* that they have learnt to make better. In this way, if you see yourself as a food lover, you must come to Kazakhstan and its most beautiful city, the culinary capital, that is Alma-Ata. Here you will learn what 'to enjoy your food' really means. Here you will find the spirit of the heroes of Rabelais, Dumas and Marquez who at one time sang the praises of this form of enjoyment. But you had better hurry if you want to find genuinely divine food. Why? Well, read on.

JUST DON'T PANIC: YOU HAVE BEEN INVITED FOR DINNER

In the early 1990s, when Kazakhstan was a kind of *terra incognita* for the rest of the world, travel guides (the aim of which was to warn the tourist of potential dangers) contained such remarks on our country as: beware, aggressive hospitality!

Indeed, the Kazakhs are hospitable on three fronts. First of all, they are like the ancient resident of steppe-land Eurasia, for whom a guest was not only a guest but also a carrier of information, a kind of walking CNN, bearing the latest news over the steppe. Second, they are like residents of the East, for whom the guest was a sacred thing. Third, they are simply Kazakhs, for whom hospitality and the culture of feasting is a part of the national psyche and the foundation of their civilization. And what is a feast without a respected guest? And what if this guest is a foreigner to boot?

Naturally, armed with such information and on receipt of an invitation to a Kazakh feast, or *toi*, you will panic just by thinking about the volume of dishes and the insistence of the hosts, whom it is difficult to refuse when they ask you to try every single dish put before you. The matter is worsened if you are invited to celebrate an official occasion, such as a wedding, the birth of a child, an anniversary, birthday, etc. If you are frightened, then generally speaking your reaction is justified. Not even native Kazakhs can always manage to cope with such a volume of food that is laid out for an ordinary meal. Therefore, here you will find a number of practical pieces of advice to help you avoid finding yourself in a difficult position, particularly the following day.

The toi begins with a cold starter. At this point you should remember clearly that this is but a sort of preamble to the hot dishes to follow. Therefore, however tempting the multitude of plentiful snacks may appear, especially the delicacies, you must remember that other filling dishes are soon to appear. Kazakhs themselves are always mindful of this and therefore limit the amount of cold food they eat. It is especially difficult for foreign guests to hold back; they are usually tempted by the black and red caviar, the noble fish, the aromatic flat cakes, the meat delicacies, fowl and salads. The salads are not the kind that European cuisine has led you to expect. Kazakh salads are very filling and spicy and they are designed to stimulate the appetite and provoke renewed interest in the huge array of dishes on your table.

Kazakh cuisine is accessible to all. There is no place here for religious prejudices and preconceptions. For example, as such, Kazakhs have nothing against pork, although they do not parade the fact and they eat it only seldom, in the form of sausages and dried delicacies–a result of their association with Russians and Europeans. In turn, they trained their Russian compatriots to grow accustomed to horse meat, which traditionally they were loathe to do. To conceal the awkwardness of a situaton, when Kazakhs are forced to eat pork (at times with relish), the following joke was introduced: to the question, 'Do you eat pork?', the answer to follow is, 'Yes, if it's kosher' (or halal). Amazingly, this joke or excuse was adopted by our Jewish friends, of which there are many in Kazakhstan. In this way, pork, under the pretence of it being kosher or sanctified was covertly and unofficially admitted into Kazakhstani cuisine.

The accessibility of the Kazakh table is in contrast to the situation with regard to alcoholic beverages. Their absence on the table may be taken by guests as an insult or, at the least, as a sign of a lack of respect. In no way do the Kazakhs share the absurd prejudice of residents of the Middle East against alcoholic drinks. They point to the fact (if, in the unlikely event a theological argument arises and we do not actually recall one ever arising) and rightly so, that the Prophet actually says nothing about a ban . . ., and there then follows a long list of drinks that you can see on the shelves of any wine store.[7]

By combining plentiful and rich food with alcohol, you risk developing problems with your stomach or liver the next day. Therefore, we advise that the lion's share of the alcohol be drunk during the first batch of dishes, and then only moderate amounts thereafter. As a result of long-standing contact with the Russians, Kazakhs have come to know well that their heavy meat-based food goes down well specifically with vodka. Therefore, the Kazakhs have copied Russian culture with regard to vodka consumption (meaning it is drunk only chilled, in small shot glasses, accompanied by salted or pickled snacks and it is downed in one), and we have not regretted the fact. Therefore, both Russians and Kazakhs are shocked when they see how guests from the West take their vodka, pouring it into a glass (warm!) like whisky and then slowly sipping it. If the guest then proceeds to add ice to the glass, you can expect to see total astonishment on the faces of the hosts (diluting vodka with water is almost considered a crime against the state).

You do not have to travel to Kazakhstan to learn how to drink vodka; spending time in Russia itself will be enough. The situation at the Kazakh table may become more complicated for you if you prefer light and more delicate drinks. They will be on the table, but during the course of the evening and as you begin to lose control over yourself (and there is a real danger of this, as this is precisely the aim that the hospitable hosts have set themselves in relation to you), you are in danger of mixing very different drinks, which is

---

[7] And so it is that Mohammed could know nothing of, say, whisky or gin. All he knew was wine (*sharap* in Arabic) and a distilled drink called *arak* (today this word in Kazakh and other Eastern languages means vodka). Arak is also the name given to an aniseed-flavoured strong liquor.

considered the greatest tragedy among post-Soviet people. If you have wisely decided to follow the example of others and stick to vodka, do not be tempted to drink your vodka down with koumiss to dampen its harsh taste. Indeed, koumiss is ideal for this: in a moment the bitter taste of the spirit will be replaced by a pleasant aroma, especially if you have tried a piece of dried horse meat. However, be careful! Being a fermented drink itself, koumiss rapidly starts to play by its own rules and very soon you will feel its effect on your stomach.

So, you have got through the first part of the meal. After a pause comes the next wave of dishes. As a minimum, two sets of hot dishes are served at the Kazakh table. If you find yourself at a toi to celebrate a major event, be prepared for still more dishes. There is one other piece of advice you should heed at this point: choose only one from the two or more hot dishes, which is more to your liking. It is most likely that one of them will be the already familiar Beshbarmak. If you have come to love the abundance of meats in a hot and spicy broth (*sorpa*), that is what you can stick with. Combined with beshbarmak, vodka will present no danger.

If you favour elegant Eastern dishes, we recommend you choose plov. This dish is familiar to Europeans in name (like pilaf) from Turkish and Persian cuisine, but the Kazakh version differs greatly. Kazakh plov also differs from the Uzbek or Tajik versions, which are considered to be the classic dish. However, unlike the dish from the two southerly neighbours from whence this treat first came, the Kazakhs sometimes use fine chickpeas (*nohat*) and coloured rice, although the preference is for white rice and, most importantly, meat, which our settled neighbours use more frugally. The great thing about plov made with rice is that the body digests it easily, although at first glance the dish may appear greasy. Plov goes well with a dry wine but has no objection to stronger drinks either.

At the Kazakh table, be prepared to be asked to make a toast. Moreover, as you are a person who has come from a far away, you are seen as an honoured and respected guest. This means that you will be one of the first to be given the floor after the elders (*aksakals*),[8] parents and other representatives of the older

[8] This word, which is Turkic in origin, literally means 'white beard' and has been adopted into the languages of other countries, including Russian.

generation. Taking the floor, you should remember the basic principles of Eastern etiquette. You should express sincere gratitude for the chance to be present at this special occasion and for being allowed to speak. Then, you should carefully complement the host family, the Kazakh people and Kazakhstan as a whole. However, in doing this you should be most diplomatic and sincere, as Kazakhs, like no other, have an acute sense for falsehood and insincerity.

If in your speech you choose to compare the Kazakhs with their regional neighbours, portraying your hosts in a favourable light, try to be as subtle and delicate as you can. In so doing you will win over the hearts of your hosts and cause no offence to anyone. The concluding point of your toast will be a heartfelt wish for health and success to the persons responsible for the celebration and the hosts, in a language they understand – Russian or, better still, Kazakh.[9] You can be sure of a rapturous response. From this moment on, although prior to this you were unlikely to have been ignored, you will now be made a total fuss of. Therefore, be careful with your drinks and your toasts.

The final stage of such an occasion is the tea-drinking ceremony. There is nothing particular about this, apart from the the fact that the hosts round off the event and thank their guests. Sometimes, by this time, the alcohol has been removed from the table. It is possible that you will be thanked personally. If you still have space in your stomach, we advise that you drink some tea, which will help with your digestion and sober you up. Tea is usually served in three ways: black, with milk or green. Here, you should be guided by your own taste alone. As a rule, there is no coffee but, should you surprise your hosts and ask for it, it is possble they will make it for you, but in your own interests it is best to do without. Combined with the fact that you have been eating and drinking all evening, coffee will not work in your favour.

Unfortunately, in recent years this culture of luxurious and plentiful celebrations has seen a decline, as have many other aspects of the traditional Kazakh life-style. Following the modernization of the twentieth century and then, after acquiring independence

---

[9] In Kazakh this expression will sound like 'Sol ushin alyp koyaik'. You should practise, as it is really not easy to say. At a pinch you would get away with the traditional Russian 'Za zdoroviye' ('Your good health!').

and seeing the spread of a Western life-style, the discipline of a market economy, combined with the realization that there are other ways of spending their money, the Kazakhs now tend to have guests round less frequently. The younger generation, unlike their grandparents and parents, have no interest in spending an enormous amount of time and effort in preparing food and then washing the dishes. However, it should be noted that the younger generation is still keen when it comes to taking up an invitation to attend such events as guests. So, at best, a celebratory dinner may well be hosted at a restaurant which offers national cuisine.

However, when the crucial moment comes (parents' anniversary, birth of children, the marriage of younger brothers and sisters, etc.) the representatives of the new market-oriented generation do feel the pinch, but they do mark the occasion in the proper way. The older generation act as examiners here, and there has not been an occasion where they have been left disappointed. However, time inexorably moves on, so if you wish to attend a genuine Eastern feast, you had better hurry.

So, you have been invited to a genuine Kazakh feast. May the Lord watch over you!

THE NATIONAL PSYCHOLOGY: ETIQUETTE, HIERARCHY AND THE FAMILY

As we all know, there is nothing worse than finding yourself in an awkward situation in an unknown environment. Therefore, when setting out for Kazakhstan, you should remember that etiquette and the social structure evolved over time and was subject to many external influences. There are occasions when old traditions and customs force your companions in conversation to do and say one thing, while their own experience and upbringing prompt them to do and say something else. With this in mind it is important for you to decode the message sent to you by your companions in conversation.

If you master a few simple rules, you will easily find your way through everyday as well as unexpected situations. First of all, you need to know that traditional Kazakh etiquette is based on and developed from rules that are generally accepted in the East, although it has its own inherently Kazakh nuances. Eastern politeness is not just empty noise and it is not hypocrisy. Everything that you are offered is not just a simple matter of politeness, as is often the case in the West, but a natural striving to oblige a guest or even just a passer-by on the street. Therefore, a refusal may be taken as a sign of a lack of respect or, worse still, as an insult. However, in any event, you will be given no indication if that is the case. In ancient times in the East, a guest who incorrectly interpreted a message concealed in a gift could have been beheaded (although he would nevertheless remain a valued guest).[10]

Perhaps Eastern politeness to guests is based on a lack of understanding and knowledge of the precise place held by a given guest in his own herarchical system. But we are only guessing. In earlier times, the attitude to uninvited guests was sensitive to a fault. So, when, in the nineteenth century the Central Asian khanates resolved to follow the route taken by Qing China and isolate themselves from the outside world, they introduced the custom of beheading all wrongdoers who tried to penetrate the borders of their emirates. At that time, many English soldiers in neghbouring British India took great interest in the ancient architectural monuments of Bukhara, Khiva and Samarkand. The inexorable draw to see these architectural masterpieces prompted them to risk their lives to visit the region. For many these journeys ended in sorrow.[11] Only the famous Arminius (Hermann Vambery), arriving in Khiva with a Kazakh caravan, was able to trick his hospitable hosts and stay alive, thanks to his brilliant knowledge of Arabic and Persian and all the Turkic dialects. After these lands were joined to the Russian Empire, Europeans visiting Turkestan were as safe here as if they were strolling the Champs-Elysees or Piccadilly.

But these are all cases of days long gone. If foreigners face a threat in Central Asia nowadays, it is to have a purse or camera stolen. To ensure this does not happen, if you are travelling on your own, in addition to the usual safety guidelines, heed the advice of your Kazakh friends. Usually, such advice is essentially focused on not displaying excessive independence and curiosity where you are not asked to do so.

---

[10] This is reminiscent of a situation when a titled signor was beheaded in medieval Europe. Even at the moment of execution he always retained his rank of duke, count, marquis, etc.

[11] So, in Bukhara in 1840, Captain Connolly (an Irishman, incidentally) gave up his life. There were also other victims of the British interest in this region on the eve of its conquering by Russia.

But enough of Eastern politeness. Let us move on to Kazakh etiquette. First of all it is built entirely on the principal of seniority. Wherever you happen to be in Kazakh society, there will always be one respected gentleman of venerable age. He will be shown marked signs of respect by the other members of the company gathered there and you should follow their example. For example, this means shaking his hand as a greeting with both palms. In conversation, you should never interrupt under any circumstances and attend closely to what he is saying, nodding your head, even if you have not understood a thing. This *aksakal* will be seated in the place of honour (the *torge*), usually opposite the main entrance. Do not be surprised if you find yourself fulfilling the role of the aksakal. If this does happen, try to behave appropriately, saying little, again thoughtfully nodding, as if approving something, and maintain a meaningful silence.

In the course of this encounter you will be served tea. If you feel you have had enough, move your cup (or teabowl) forward about 10–20cm and hold the palm of your hand over it for a couple of seconds. This gesture is sufficient; it will not go unnoticed and you will no longer be offered endless cups of tea.

There may be an instance where a gathered company contains both a gentleman of venerable age and a person who is younger, but who occupies a prominent place in society. In this instance, the outward priority is given to the elder man, to whom the big boss will show clear marks of respect. However, he will also enjoy marks of respect when he is addressed by the others. You should act as the others do. Where necessary, you should tactfully show this person that you understand his true position in the social hierarchy; your personal reputation will only grow as a result.

Women in Kazakh society, be it traditional or contemporary society, are afforded considerable attention. Female representatives of the elder generation are shown the same marks of respect as their male counterparts. Moreover, many women who have raised children, grandchildren and great-grandchildren feel like matrons in any Kazakh company. As sovereign ladies of the family or clan they secretly demand attention that is befitting of their status and they receive it, too, perhaps with a feeling that is even more sincere than that afforded to the old men. It is probably a case of every Kazakh seeing their own mother or grandmother in these matron-like figures.

This means that Kazakh women possess certain behavioural stereotypes in regard to their men of any generation. As a result the latter have reflexes, developed in such a way that they are automatically forced to implement commands and orders of the elder women in a most obedient manner. Whatever the context, given that such reflexes are instructive, Kazakh men always respond obediently and respectfully to the commanding voices of other matronly figures – regardless.

However, all this does not mean that Kazakh men are pathetic little creatures held firmly under the thumb of their women. Most likely, their relationships are similar to those within large family clans in southern Italy, where the home, the household and family budget are controlled by the eldest signora, in years and standing. Love of 'Mummy' is intertwined with respect and deference, and a certain degree of fear. Such is the demographic situation for the Kazakhs that male patriarchs fail to live to an age when it is time to head a major family clan of several generations (wars and other social-demographic shocks of the twentieth century have caused their imbalance) and if they do live long enough, the shifts and changes of life and the philosophical attitude shown towards them convince them to hand over the reins to their women, whose commanding voices become louder and more forceful with age and with whom arguing becomes more and more onerous and harder to endure.

As can be imagined, this is not a situation over which Kazakhs hold a monopoly; it is much the same for all nations with a patriarchal, clan-based life-style, where the transformation to a post-traditionalist society remains incomplete. Kazakhs are famous for being master elocutionists and authors of sayings expressing wonderful meaning and imagery. All the centuries-old wisdom of relationships between men and women is reflected in the popular (among the men) Kazakh saying, which roughly translates as: if all girls are beautiful before marriage, where do the Megaera-wives come from?[12] Here, as across the world, it is customary to believe that the Kazakh men both love and revere their women. We hope that you come to share this view after closer acquaintance.

---

[12] In this regard, the following story is recalled: in the early 1990s there was a very popular Disney version of *Beauty and the Beast* out in Kazakhstan (and everywhere else for that matter). The film was accompanied by comics containing this story. Kazakh fathers read this story to their sons at bedtime, ending it with the words: 'And the beast turned into a handsome prince and they were married. Whereupon the beauty turned into a beast.'

If you find yourself in the company of Kazakhs of the same age, who grew up in Soviet times, you can consider yourself lucky. Here you may do away with conventional etiquette and hierarchy. Kazakh youth in the Brezhnev era was quite open and liberal, so it is seen as bad form to establish any hierarchical divisions or forms of selection by clan, region, property or any other criteria. If you find yourself in this environment you will feel you have been transported twenty or thirty years back in time. Be prepared to hear discussions in the style of the European intellectuals of the 1960s, on capitalism and socialism, philosophy and history, Jean-Paul Sartre and Herbert Marcuse, music and the fine arts. Then, when all has been said and discussions held in this customary spiritual and emotional blend, the children and grandchildren of the recent builders of socialism take to their Mercedes, BMWs and Hummers to return the following day to their offices and banks, refreshed and revitalized to set about the construction of an exemplary capitalist society. But that is another story.

THE NATIONAL PSYCHOLOGY: CUSTOMS AND ORIGINS

The Kazakh mentality has evolved in a very complex manner. Ancient customs and more contemporary concepts have not contradicted one another over the course of history; rather they have supplemented one another and formed layers, one on top of another. They often intertwined harmoniously, creating a wonderful blend of different concepts which present in their totality a certain well-structured philosophical system to explain the world they inhabit.

From the very outset, when the Kazakhs first entered the historical stage, the rest of the world was not particularly friendly towards them. In fact, quite the opposite. Therefore, their customs formed in a way that would ensure the nation's survival. The basis of the nation was the clan, a kind of expanded version of the family. The clan and the family, in turn, was formed by the generations, one replacing the other. Therefore, the first and most sacred duty of every Kazakh is to know their ancestors, going back a minimum of seven generations, chronologically accounting for an average of from one hundred to one hundred and fifty years.

However, the majority of Kazakhs hold more extensive information on their origins. This is possible thanks to a largely mythological system with a genealogical tree, well established in the nation's consciousness, and in which every clan and every tribe is represented. Knowing the last seven generations, any Kazakh will readily find his clan on this tree. At its base sits the legendary Alash, the mythical forefather of all Kazakhs. As such, every clan has the same forefather to whom they trace their origins. Perhaps some of these mythical characters were in fact real people. Sometimes the founding father is replaced by an animal, which becomes a totem for the clan. For Kazakhs, as with other Turks, this is generally the wolf (or the she-wolf). In this way, we see that traditional Kazakh mythology is very reminiscent of the ancient legends of many other peoples of Eurasia, primarily of their nomadic neighbours. However, parallels are sometimes detected with more distant peoples (as evidenced graphically by the legend of the she-wolf that reared the progenitor). In this case it is with the Romans.

Ancestral memory and ancestral links, therefore, had an important and defining significance for the Kazakhs because they ensured the principal objective of surviving in a hostile environment. Members of different clans had to help one another, protect one another and come to one another's aid. All of this was held together by strong kindred relationships.[13] During wartime, and wartime was the usual state of affairs for the militant Turkic nomads in ancient times, every clan automatically transformed itself into a fighting unit, something between a regiment and a division. All the armies of the great conquerors of Eurasia were based very much on this type of tribal structure for their troops. Perhaps this is what explains the triumphant nature of the invincible Tumens[14] of Chinggis Khan.

The entire social structure of the Kazakhs and other nomadic Turks had a clearly expressed militarized nature. Their neighbours adopted this structure from them, having proved their vitality in conditions of constant war and forays. So, practically with no change at all, their neighbours the Ukrainian and the Russian

---

[13] In this connection an old joke comes to mind about a Kazakh sent to the Moon by the Soviet space programme. While other cosmonauts were studying the lunar landscape, the Kazakh began running. Asked why by his surprised comrades, the Kazakh answered that he was running to search for his relatives. They say that the Kazakh will find relatives even on the Moon.

[14] A Tumen was a combat unit of the Turko-Mongolian Army. At their peak, the Tumens numbered some 10,000 people.

Cossacks copied this militarized system from the Kazakhs, where it was adopted, as we can see, together with the way they named themselves. However, while taking the military structure from the Kazakhs, the Cossacks could not adopt the system of family and clan relations.

In more recent times, the clan links continued to play an important role in the social lives of the Kazakhs. As the steppe came to know times of peace it was economic relations and interests that came to the fore. In such circumstances, the clan system acquired a new objective – namely, the accumulation and accrual of clan riches in the form of livestock and pasture land. The clans inevitably began to compete among themsleves for pastures and water sources, for control over caravan routes and so on. In such conditions, the clan system helped in establishing family relationships, finding compromises and making mutually-beneficial exchanges with regard to disputed holdings.

Of course, this system should not be seen in absolute terms. It was far from being as harmonious as all that, as it appears through the prism of time. There was great inequality in terms of property within a single clan, the aristrocracy ignored the rights of the ordinary members of the clan who sometimes resorted to violence in pursist of their rights. Nevertheless, over the course of their history, the Kazakhs always knew and valued their clan identity.

The stormy events of the twentieth century proved that belonging to a clan is a cornerstone of the Kazakh identity. Clan relationships were challenged even back in the era of Tsarist Russia, in the latter half of the nineteenth century. Some Kazakhs were drawn into industrial production; they left their native auls and resettled in the cities. Some even deserted their native steppes and went to search for a living away from their native Kazakhstan, to the industrial centres of Russia and Siberia. Nevertheless, members of a clan did try to help one another and, when needed, to support a fellow member of their tribe. This factor considerably simplified the lives of the unprotected members of society: the orphans, the young and inexperienced, the sick, the elderly and the lonely, etc.

However, the real break-up in the traditional system occurred after the Revolution and in the process of the modernization of Kazakhstan. As a result of all the social and demographic upheavals in the middle of the twentieth century it seemed to many observers that the traditional social structures of the Kazakhs had been destroyed for good. However, they proved their longevity and primacy in the form of a national memory. It is possible that this was one of the manifestations of a survival instinct of the Kazakhs as a nation. One way or another, though, the memory of family connections, which played but a symbolic role in the Soviet era, lived on for the entire duration of the era of violent Soviet modernization.

With independence came the chance for the Kazakhs to revive former tribal links, at least in the form of historical tradition. Information on the Kazakhs' clan structure came to be openly published (something banned in Soviet times) and it was discussed across society and in the media. However, the resistance of the ruling class to the attempts to revive the division of the Kazakhs on a Zhuz [horde] and clan basis was steadfast.[15] From the standpoint of Soviet tradition which promoted such views as the manifestation of 'feudal, clan-based antiquity', such behaviour of the Kazakh elite, which was embedded in the Soviet bureacracy, would have been completely logical. However, this is actually not what happened.

The new ruling class, which took over the reigns of power in Kazakhstan after the ignominious fall of the Soviet regime, was faced with the task of building a nation-state, in which *a priori* there was no place for any division by clan principle. Attempts to divide the people of Kazakhstan by ethnic origin or religion were also firmly suppressed. Instead, the concept of a 'single Kazakhstani nation' was proposed.[16] Today, it is hard to imagine how a single nation could be moulded from so many different ethnic groups. Even American society could not cope with such a task, where in place of the earlier, 'melting pot' concept came the offer of the 'salad pot' theory.

It is likely that much will depend on the spirit, the will and the ethnic composition of the elite that is currently taking shape. Today, it is represented mostly by Kazakhs, who have adopted a consolidating role in the building of a new nation. It cannot be

---

[15] The Zhuz was a union of tribes and clans in the Kazakh khanate. There were three principal Zhuzes, or Hordes, as they are better known: the Great, Middle and Small Hordes. The division of the Hordes coincided in terms of both composition and territory; on the one hand, with the territorial and administrative division of the Turkic states, sequentially replacing one another within Kazakhstan, while on the other hand, with economic and geographical zones, defining the routes and the radius of the nomadic wandering.

[16] Instead of the term 'Kazakh' one suggestion was to use the term 'Kazakhstani'.

ruled out that in future Kazakhstan will embrace the concept of multiculturalism, which is now the subject of considerable debate in the West. But for now, Kazakh society is held together by the general, although visibly erosive, Soviet-wide mentality of different ethnic groups.

As far as the traditional understanding of Kazakh clan affiliations is concerned, another delicate matter arises. Foreign observers and researchers of Kazakhstan have pointed to the fact that Kazakh bureacracy apparently functions and is formed on the clan principle. They then transferred this view to post-Soviet Kazakhstan. At the heart of this perception lay the methodology of Western social anthropology, tested against the example of certain traditional societies of the post-colonial world. However, the more attentive researchers of contemporary Kazakhstani society very logically point to the fact that the formation of a new ruling class and a new political and economic elite is by no means developing on the basis of clan-based generality or belonging to some clan or locality.

It is obvious, therefore, that there are other mechanisms at work. They are closer, it would appear, to those that were in play in Western European societies during the first industrial revolution. It is all to do with the way economic interests unite people, not in terms of family allegiances, but on the basis of a common striving towards success.

As far as the place and the role of the clan mentality in the life of the Kazakhs is concerned, practically any Kazakh will answer your question regarding clan relationships to the best of his ability. He could tell you of his geographical origins and, more accurately, of his clan and its history. Then he will tell you of his family ties that bind him with other members of society. On occasion he may joke about other Kazakh clans, each of which holds a specific function in popular folklore, or has certain weaknesses and strange characteristics. But he will never tell you how his belonging to a certain clan has promoted, for example, his progression at work or his financial successes. All that is left is for you to content yourself with indeterminate rumours and unverified information. (See the next section for more on the hordes.)

However, you do have the chance to learn to what extent the legends of the Kazakhs' clan system correspond with reality. For this you have to enter from within, meaning you have to become related, marry or be adopted; you have to become a member of this clan. Only then and only after many, many years have past, when your children and perhaps your grandchildren have grown up as genuine Kazakhs, will you start to understand how the mechanism of the Kazakhs' close congenic relations really works. But no sooner. However, love and marriage, to which we will return, will be considered later.

AND SOMETHING ELSE ABOUT THE TRADITIONAL KAZAKH SYSTEM

It is impossible to understand anything in Kazakh history and modern development without delving into the history of the horde and tribal systems.

Historical tradition has identified quite specific functions relating to each horde. It is assumed that the Small Horde was responsible for the security of the Kazakh Khanate and protected the western and south-western borders of the Khanate. The symbol of this horde is the spear. Indeed, it is the representatives of this horde that were famed for their warlike nature, when other tribes had moved over to peaceful livestock breeding. They siezed the territory of the Mangyshlak (Mangystau) Peninsula, which today is the basis of the country's oil riches, from the Kazakhs' neighbours, the Turkmen, earlier famed for their ferocity and warring nature. Furthermore, they were the most merciless slave traders and raiders of the caravans. Their regular forays on neighbours from the north, subjects of the Russian Empire, were to a great extent the reason for Russian expansion into Kazakh lands. All the qualities and vices of the Small Horde were concentrated in the Adai tribe whose name became legendary in the region and beyond. According to the Kazakh saying, built on a play on words: In Heaven there is Kudai [God]; on Land there is Adai.

The privilege of intellectual work was a tradition preserved for the Middle Horde, securing it the symbol of the quill. This meant that representatives of the horde were to work as officials, writers and poets. Indeed, by amazing chance, it was people from this horde who were to become the founders and creators of classical Kazakh literature. In Soviet times it was these people who made up the creative and scientific intelligentsia. The most well-known of the tribes from this Middle Horde were the Kipchaks and the Argyns. At one time the Kipchaks occupied a leading position in the Great Steppe from Pamir to the Carpathians; they are better known to Europeans as Kumans and, after Napoleon, as Mamluks. This was one of few Kazakh tribes, subjected to minimal Mongolization. Their fragmented descendants populate Turkey, the Crimea, Hungary, Lithuania, Egypt, the Caucasus, the Volga and Urals regions, Siberia and Central Asia. However, the greatest numbers were preserved in the native steppe land which for centuries in world historiography was known in Persian as Desht-i-Kipchak (the land of the Kipchaks).

The other clan of the Middle Horde were the Argyns, the largest tribe in terms of numbers among the Kazakhs, who accounted for almost half of all Kazakhs living in the country. Their origin is shrouded behind a curtain of history. They appeared centre stage quite unexpectedly and became the most numerous of the population of the Kazakh steppe. This occurred on numerous occasions in the history of the Turks, when the latest favourite united other tribes around it and gave them its name. However, with the Argyns this was the last instance and they were not able to impose their name on other clans. And this is how they exist today: dominant, but not controlling. The women of this clan are known for their indomitable spirit and life force. With other Kazakh clans there was once an unspoken ban (more precisely a recommendation, secured in the corresponding saying) on taking an Argyn as a wife. It was fashionable for the older generation of Kazakhs to marry Tatars or Russians. A rather painful scar in the memory of the Kazakhs was for some reason left by Tatar women related by blood, language and customs, although they did bestow on their descendants blond hair and blue eyes. Their grandchildren, now living in the Brezhnev era and imbued with Kazakh patriotism, would take Kazakh women as brides on a matter of principle. Naturally, the largest contingent was made up of wonderful Argyn girls, who had retained their ideal steppe beauty in its original form. However, when marrying, these young men, who had grown up in an urban environment, gradually came to understand the wisdom of their grandfathers. All that is left to say by way of consolation is that the Argyn women do pass on to their descendants an indomitable will to live and to survive. This is how the unfulfilled *passionarity* of this people is expressed, a people to a great extent artificially included in the composition of the Kazakh nation but which has not become the forefather of a nation of its own.

And finally there is the Great Horde. A popular saying has it in the most esteemed of roles, the symbol of which is a rod (or more correctly, a staff). It means the role of a shepherd or pastor, not in a spiritual sense but in a worldly sense. The function of this horde was to control and to direct. In Tsarist times this function was not manifested, probably because the Great Horde was joined to the empire last. However, in the Soviet period the concealed talent of this association of the most ancient of clans (some of which appeared here when Europe was under the Republic of Rome, i.e. before the Common Era) blossomed with luxuriant colour. The upper layer of the Kazakh Soviet bureaucratic establishment was recruited as a rule from the representatives of this horde. Any attempts by representatives of other tribes to penetrate this upper category of power ended in failure. It cannot be said that Moscow made any conscious effort by way of policy to favour the Great Horde in particular. Most likely, Moscow simply did not suspect the existence of this horde system among the Kazakhs or they saw it as the vestiges of a distant past.

In the post-Soviet era, the traditional roles of the hordes and tribes began to die out, although attentive observers have noted that they have not disappeared altogether. It is unclear on what principle financial riches are accumulated in modern-day Kazakhstan. If *Forbes* magazine is to be believed, Kazakhstan supplies billionnaires to the world: mostly Jews, Koreans and Indians, but not Kazakhs.

THE NATIONAL PSYCHOLOGY: DREAMS AND PREJUDICES

As we have seen, the Kazakh national psychology has been forged over time under the strong influence of a traditional value system. However, new influences, like the modern-day way of life, have had a major impact on them, too.

In the old days there used to be a less than kindly joke, for which the Kazakhs are obliged to their derisive neighbours (probably the Tatars). The joke goes as follows: if a Russian gets rich, he will buy himself a cow; if an Uzbek (or a Sart in the original[17]) gets rich, he will build himself another house; if a Kazakh gets rich, he will take himself another wife. The joke, infact, bears witness not so much to

[17] *Sart* is how the nomads so contemptuously called their agrarian neighbours. After the creation of the Soviet republics of Central Asia in the 1920s, the Sarts, the Iranian- and Turkic-speaking population of the Fergana Valley and Maverennahr, took the ancient and proud name of 'Uzbek'. This is how the Turkic-speaking Sarts in Chinese Turkestan acted, who called themselves 'Taranchi'. They adopted the ancient name and came to be known as 'Uygurs'. What is most surprising is that over the course of the twentieth century they really did develop into new nations. Both the former and the latter cannot stand the Kazakhs, who they unsuccessfully try to see as lower than themselves in a cultural and historical context.

the popularity of polygamy among the Kazakhs and not to the hyper-sexual tendencies of this nation. What it speaks of is the presence of an institution of status; on the importance of social status for the Kazakhs, something that was determined to a great extent by the number of households. Each household is a separate yurta [nomad's tent], a separate herd and a separate family. This means that a well-established polygamist was a potential forefather of a new clan. And this is a ticket to the train of history. However, there were also poorly-established polygamists among the Kazakhs. We have spoken already about the relationship of the Kazakhs to their iron-willed wives. And, on the whole, this relationship was not particularly good at promoting the blossoming of polygamy!

And so, in their dreams and prejudices, the Kazakhs always devoted much attention to the issue of status. To occupy a place just a little bit higher was the cherished dream of every dweller of the steppe. In the traditional hierarchy it was physically impossible to rise to the very top: all vacant places in the prestigious clans, the Tore and the Kozha, were taken by the descendants of Chinggis Khan and the Prophet Mohammed. Therefore, the simple Kazakhs set about creating their own hierarchy and a new aristocracy, consisting of wise lawmakers, gallant leaders and individuals (*batyrs*) and zealous organizers of the economy (*bais*). All of this new aristocracy submitted to the traditional authorities, the sultans and the khans, with extreme reluctance.

After the Russians came and after the establishment of a Russian administrative system in the Kazakh steppe, many Kazakhs happily rushed to find employment in Russian organizations, where they could receive the high social status they cherished and therefore stand out from their fellow tribesmen. This process had a serious, positive effect: by the early twentieth century Kazakh society had a powerful intellectual streak of specialists in the most varied of spheres, educated in the European style. After the Revolution, the Kazakhs found that they had to start all over again in many areas. But here, too, the striving to assert oneself in the new hierarchical system was also manifested. However, on this occasion the price was high: the Stalinist purges in the spirit of *nativization*[18] of the bureaucratic apparatus regularly created vacant spaces, to be filled by new victims.

[18] Localization (nativization) was an official policy in the USSR, directed to preparing Soviet and party personnel in the national republics.

In the second half of the twentieth century, in addition to the position held, new stimuli and new status symbols appeared: place of residence (capital), car, dacha, academic diploma, etc. Occasionally, somewhere in the far south, in neglected villages, polygamists could still be found; followers of traditional symbols of status. After the fall of the Soviet system in 1991, everything changed radically. The Kazakhs, just like other nations of the socialist bloc, came up against the challenge presented by possessions representing status and prestige, recognized by the entire world. At first, the new Kazakh elite eyed the owners of luxury cars and yachts, villas and palaces, designer clothes and Swiss watches with wonder and envy. Privatization and the new economic order enabled some of them very soon to touch this world of luxury, but they became none the happier for it.

Others dreamed not of symbols of material status but of actual prosperity. This means the power and economic might that were held by familiar leaders of the globalized economy, heads of major corporations and banks. This category of Kazakhs set about creating a similar world in their own back yard, simulating a pseudo-globalized social hierarchy. If in the West the 'nouveau Kazakhs' had managed to establish strong relations and had forced others to acknowledge them as part of the 'Brave New World', at home, where in no time they created whole new cities, entire sections of industry, a wonderful banking system, a completely new mass media and where they flooded the market with state-of-the-art goods, they remained the same as they had been, both for themselves and for others: young people who had grown up in modest conditions and who had been raised in families with a harsh socialist psychology.

A vicious circle ensued: dreams push the 'nouveau Kazakhs' to achieve the latest heights and overcome new challenges, but it is no easy matter liberating oneself from the embraces of traditional psychology and one's own mentality. With each new page of Kazakh history, this tale repeats itself every time. Today, we observe how the traditional Kazakh identity, with its strange prejudices and naïve delusions, encounters once again the challenge of the present. However, there is almost no doubt that, as in the past, it will remain on its feet; it will experience yet another breakdown of social relations, then revisit the previous value system, based on close congeneric and marital, brotherly and amicable links and which, in essence, is democratic, plethoric and vibrant. When this cycle ends, for whatever reason, then the Kazakhs will end their existence, too.

THE NATIONAL PSYCHOLOGY: SELF-EXPRESSION, MUSIC AND ART

Kazakhstan's visual arts have a long history, despite the fact that in their contemporary form they only began to develop in the twentieth century. In the first millennium before the Common Era, the tribes of Sakas, populating the territory of Kazakhstan, started to make cave drawings of animals, warriors, chariots, battle scenes and hunting images. The cave painting of the Sakas, known to us through the famous depictions in the Tamgaly Tract, was closely linked with their way of life, half-nomadic and half-settled and distributed in the main in South and East Kazakhstan.

The second stage in the development of the visual genre began with the advent of the ancient Turks at the end of the first millennium before the Common Era and in the early first millennium of the Common Era. The Turks adopted the bases of wall-painting techniques from their Saka ancestors, which found expression in the creation of runic script. Monuments of this culture became widespread across an enormous territory, encompassing Mongolia, Siberia, Altai and south-east Kazakhstan. In the era of the early Turks in the first millennium, Buddhism and Christianity (Manichaeism and Nestorianism) reached Kazakhstan and they also found their artistic expression on walls, in stone and in architecture. The images of Buddha in the River Ili Basin near Alma-Ata are particularly impressive. These grand figures are made with considerable artistry. Alongside Buddhism, the Indian and Chinese painting styles also penetrated into Central Asia.

After the year 751 Islam was strengthened in Kazakhstan. In the Muslim era Iranian miniatures became popular with the Turks of Central Asia who had conquered the oases of Bukhara and Samarkand and advanced into Afghanistan and Iran. At the same time, Islam forbade images of humans and animals.

After the formation of the Kazakh Khanate in the fifteenth century, decorative art with the characteristic ornamental pattern became widespread across the entire territory of Kazakhstan. This ornamental pattern served to decorate the traditional Kazakh dwelling, the yurta, festive dress, musical instruments, weapons, crockery and so on. In style it originates from the so-called 'animal style' of the Saka tribes, in which the symbols of a ram's horns and other animals appear in different forms.

In the nineteenth century, European painting became famous in Central Asia thanks to Russian settlers, Polish and Ukrainian political exiles and German, French and English travellers, geographers and naturalists. In the mid-nineteenth century, some members of the Kazakh intelligentsia, such as Chokan Valikhanov, a European-educated academic, endeavoured to copy Western graphic art and pastel work.

In the twentieth century, painting developed in Kazakhstan under the strong influence of European art. Classical European and academic Russian painting had a strong impact on the Kazakhstani artists. From the 1930s to the 1950s Kazakhstani painting was dominated by Socialist Realism. In the latter half of the twentieth century, many Kazakhstani artists were greatly influenced by styles such as Impressionism, Post-Impressionism, Cubism, Avantgardism and Mannerism. This process saw active development from the 1950s to the 1970s.

In the 1970s and 1980s, a new generation of artists entered Kazakhstan graphic art and their aesthetic ideals were of a clearly-defined nationalistic nature. The painting technique and the subject-matter begin to show an echo of their Kazakh roots. The 'New Wave' of Kazakh artists, using the techniques of the best examples of Western and Soviet painting that they knew and creating new techniques of their own, introduced elements of ancient Turkic and traditional Kazakh ornamentalist techniques into their creative work. The subjects treated also had a strong propensity towards national history. A philosophical calling to nature was widespread in the paintings of this period, which was also closely linked with the specific nature of the traditional nomadic way of life of the Kazakhs.

Today, in independent Kazakhstan, this generation of masters makes up the core of famous artists. Their work graces many of the world's picture galleries. The President of the Republic, too, has decorated his new residence with pictures by these artists. At the same time, in recent years, under the influence of the latest technologies and computer graphics, new genres and styles are being developed in Kazakhstan.

And yet the Kazakhs' principal art form was not painting. As the Kazakhs' ancestors, being nomads, did not have such art forms as visual arts, architecture, choreography and so on, they developed an extraordinary sense of hearing and of smell, such as is the case with the blind. In other words, the Kazakhs perfected their skills in music and the oral arts. Clearly, it is from here that the Kazakhs get their ability to master foreign languages, a trait that has been noticed by many. It would appear that Kazakhs approach the study of foreign dialects as they would the imitation of a new type of music.

The Kazakhs perfected their predilection for lampooning, metaphors, mockery, figurative comparison and other poetic expressions. The expression 'rather lose a friend than a jest' suits them perfectly. Any Kazakh had a talent for augmenting thoughts and feelings with expressive imagery; every aul had its literary champion, an inveterate wit and a part-time jester.

Once a season or once a year, depending upon the significance of the event being held, a kind of competition would be arranged for such wits on a regional and national scale and it was given the name *aitys*. The participants would poke fun at each other, at an opponent's clan and at the important political events of the day; they would recall past exploits, celebrate their women and racehorses and glorify their ancestral line. The winner received a valuable prize and it so happened that great riches could be taken away at the end of such a competition. However, as a rule, these wandering minstrels and bards were not dependent upon material riches; their wealth quickly evaporated in the same way it was obtained – on feasting. However, the songs and eulogies they composed at the aitys lived on and the best were carried across the steppe and became a part of the national heritage.

On a domestic level this is what would happen. A weary traveller, having covered hundreds of kilometres over the unpopulated steppe and finally reaching a godforsaken aul, just about manages to get off his horse, which itself is barely able to stand up. According to all the canons of Kazakh hospitality he would first be fed and then allowed to rest. The second phase would be to hear the news, imparted by the traveller (that is, if he knew anything of interest). And finally, the third phase would follow, a test of endurance or, if you like to use the Russian version, an 'inspection for lice'.[19] The guest would be slowly taunted with various jokes. One excuse could be the multitude of family ties of the Kazakhs. This means that in a formal sense the jokes and ripostes would be addressed to

[19] Incidentally, there was no problem with this in the old steppe. The witty offspring, familiar with English, even used this moment to good effect, joking that every Kazakh always has his own beat-group to hand; 'pit or bit' in Kazakh means 'louse'.

his relatives, but in reality it was intended for the guest: I recall that your cousin Sapar ran after a donkey with no owner at the bazaar and in the process had his own horse stolen. Your Aunt Nazgul got to scolding him so, and in the process she broke her new ladle over his head. And while they were quarrelling thieves ran off with the last of their belongings. And so on in the same vein.

It was usually the women who started, with the male companions in conversation possibly then joining them if the guest remained in the background and lost face. Now if, on the contrary, the guest himself proved to be an inveterate wit, the chief jester of the aul would come to the aid of his fellow villagers. If the guest were to succeed in holding his own and put the latter to shame, he would be afforded the corresponding level of respect. In fact, all of the above was a part of the social etiquette. In other contexts this could be seen in the civilized societies of Paris and St Petersburg and in high society throughout the West.

After the meal and the revelry in mutual jokes and witticisms came the musical interlude and the guest would take up the *dombra,* the Kazakh stringed folk instrument. Now he would have to prove that he was not simply full of hot air and witty words. For the Kazakhs the dombra is not just a seemingly primitive instrument made up from a shell and two strings.[20] For a Kazakh, the dombra is not just a musical instrument, however good it may be.

---

[20] Surprising though it may be, but the dombra was not the product of an anonymous popular genius. Its design and sound were developed by the ingenious Central Asian scholar, mathematician and philosopher Al-Farabi. He was born and lived in the south of what is now Kazakhstan (Farab, now Taraz). The Kazakhs and the Uzbeks argued long and hard whether he was a Kazakh or an Uzbek. Al-Farabi himself would have been most surprised to learn of these arguments. Educated in Persian and Arabic, he wrote and spoke in these languages. Al-Farabi was born among Turkic nomads, most likely the Kipchak tribe and his native language was steppe Turkic, the precursor ro Kazakh. However, he died in Baghdad. Al-Farabi's treatises were highly respected in Medieval Europe, in translations from Arabic.

Al-Farabi designed the mathematical model of the dombra so that it sounded as rich and sonorous as possible. The scholar was probably the first craftsman to make a dombra. Soon his specimens spread over the steppe and the instrument came to be incredibly popular and it has remained among the Kazakhs unchanged to this day. It is very unusual for science to come to the aid of art. We should not exclude the fact that Europe received not only philosophical treatises, but diagrams of the dombra too, which in form could have been used to design various stringed instruments, from the lute to the violin.

The dombra is a confidante, a faithful travel companion and a dear comrade, trusted with one's innermost secrets; a source of joy and a comforter for pain. With the dombra the Kazakh tells of the eternal and the marvellous, of what worries him, and of his love and his hate.

The dombra can be used not only to express personal feelings, but also to relate things that the entire nation is concerned with. There was an ancient legend that demonstrated the magic of this instrument. We know that the elder son of the great Chinggis Khan, Jochi, died in mysterious circumstances: he was found in the reeds with a broken spine (a widespread form of execution among the Mongols). The official version states that the heir to the largest ulus (domain), stretching from the east of the Kazakh steppes to the Atlantic,[21] died while out hunting. But in fact, Chinggis Khan ordered the removal of his stepson. (Jochi was born during the capture of Chinggis Khan's elder wife Börte and he was not the biological son, although the Khan adopted him and raised him like his own, albeit not a favourite son.) The reason lay in the wayward morals of Jochi, who perhaps knew of the secret of his parentage and, most importantly, placing claims to power at too early a stage. This all led to tragedy of Shakespearian proportions. Rashid al-Din relates that when the 'Master of the Universe' was informed of the execution, a miserly tear trickled down the cheek of the cruel conqueror.

Kazakh tradition interpreted this episode differently. According to legend, the malicious Jochi indeed died while out hunting, tracking a steppe onager. Concerned over his long absence and suspecting the worst, Chinggis Khan nevertheless announced that a cruel 'reward' would await the black messenger (i.e. the one to bring bad news): he would be filled to the throat with molten lead. Of course no one wished for such a fate and the threat of violent reprisal hung over whole tribes. Then an old musician volunteered to bring the dark news. Without saying a word he used the language of music to inform the great conqueror of the death of his son. Chinggis Khan understood everything from the song of the dombra. In a wild rage he ordered that the old man be executed, but officially, the old man had not said a word. So the dombra was

[21] Officially, the promised domain ended where the Mongolian horse could no longer tread; where land ended.

found to be ultimately responsible and it was filled with molten lead. The conqueror himself only outlived his unfavoured son but a short while. From that time, in memory of the tragedy that unfolded in October 1227 in the River Ili delta on the banks of Lake Balkhash, the Kazakhs place a piece of lead into the shell of every dombra. If you shake any dombra you can hear the rattle of this piece of evidence of an ancient tragedy.

The tragic and the funny are closely interwoven in Kazakh folklore. This means that, taking account of the fact that life in the old steppe was full of hardship and deprivation, humour acted as a form of self-defence, communication and support for the necessary level of human warmth and mutual understanding between fellow tribesmen, without which the spiritual life of the nation is meaningless.

Poetry went hand in hand with music and any resident of the steppe could use poetic imagery and symbols. The heavenly beauty of a girl, the majestic view of the mountains, the endless expanses of the steppe, the tender, cool oasis, the slow meandering of the river, or simply the green grass on the roadside; all this could bring a nomad to dream up poetry, which in turn would become a song, accompanied by the trusty dombra, always at their side just like their weapon. Travelling unhurriedly across the steppe and without getting off his horse, the Kazakh would take up his dombra and begin to compose a song. What about? Well, about anything at all, really. About the long road, about true friends, about the loved one waiting for him at the end of his journey, the loveliest in all the world, about dear parents, merry brothers and graceful sisters. At times this plethora of poetic improvization could yield a single musical or poetic masterpiece. An impetus could come in the form of an emotional shock, such as separation from a loved one, the death of a loved one, a cruel war, victory in a terrible battle and so on.

Kazakh poetry has its romantic and heroic tales, very much in the spirit of Romeo and Juliette, Tristan and Isolde, the exploits of the Nibelung and El Cid. In the twentieth century, having received a European education, the Kazakh students of folklore gathered a considerable part of this epic material, preserving it for posterity. Today we can listen to operas which draw on this material.

The poetic and musical traditions of the past are still very much alive and it cannot be said that they are some kind of museum exhibit or, as they say, 'ethnography in a can'. The tradition is alive

1. Folklore concert

2

2. New mosque in the new capital

3

3. Street scene in Astana

4

4. Monument of female form symbolizing 'motherland', Astana

5

5. 'The Pyramid': venue for inter-confessional and inter-ethnic congresses, Astana

6

6. Typical 'Aksakal' (White-Barber)

7

7. View of the Culture Centre, Astana

8

8. Abstract figure celebrating Kazakhstan's music traditions, Astana

9

9. Distant panorama of the old parliament, Astana

10

10. Celebrating women's festival day, Astana

11

11. Presidential building, Astana

12. View of the Baiterek Tower, Astana

13. Celebrating Victory Day (9 May): portrait of a veteran

14

14. Section of the monument dedicated to the Kazakh's ancient forbears (the Sakas)

15

15. View of Almaty (old or 'Southern' capital)

16

16. Intercontinental Hotel ('Ankara'), Almaty

17

17. Korean traditional dance

18

18. Caucasian traditional dance

19

19. A stroll in the park, Almaty

20

20. Kazakh traditional dance

21

21. Skateboarding expertise!

22

22. Almaty – city in the mountains

23

23. Back in the USSR? (the Veterans)

24

24. President Nursultan Nazarbaev (with First Lady) and Patriarch of the Orthodox Church, Almaty

25

25. Russian monks at an Orthodox Holy Day, Almaty

26

26. Easter cakes

27

27. Pumpkin harvest

28. Eurasian face of Kazakhstan

29. A 'Berkutchi' – Hawk hunter

30

30. The eternal wisdom of the Ala-Tau mountains

31

31. Wind in the desert

32

32. A 'Berkutchi' (Hawk hunter) near his yurta (traditional home)

33

33. White yurta with decorative features

34

34. Mountain lake

35

35. Bactrian camels roaming in the snow

36

36. Resort along the Ili river in the Almaty region

37

37. Kapchagay artificial lake near Almaty.

38

38. Scene along the Ili river

39

39. Enjoying the sun by the Ili river

40

40. Father and son 'Berkutchi' (hawk hunters).

41

41. The 'hawk eye' of a young 'Berkutchi'

42. Preparing for another 'lift off' at Baikonur Cosmodrome

and finds expression on almost a daily basis. You will see a dombra in every Kazakh home and at the end of a party, someone will invariably pick up the instrument to celebrate the beauty of their native land, recall the experiences of their youth, their true friends and beautiful girlfriends.

However, the instructive wit characteristic of Kazakhs is still very much alive, too, and anything could present itself as a target. It is also possible that if you commit a *faux pas* intentionally or unintentionally, no one will say anything to your face, respecting your rights as a guest, although the blunder will be discussed between the others and laughed off. The Soviet era with its sometimes absurd phenomena only served to enhance the Kazakh's natural sense of humour. However, here they were not alone and they laughed over pointless projects, grandiose public holidays, regular anniversaries, queues, food shortages and other idiocy on the part of the communist authorities, together with all the other peoples of the Soviet Union. This tradition (the tradition of political humour) has not died away and is still flourishing today. However, there is no point trying to give examples here if you do not know Russian or Kazakh, as everything is constructed on a play on words.

Nevertheless, by conversing often and at length, with the locals, you will gradually acquire an inate knowledge of local colour and nuances and, accordingly, the local sense of humour. As life continues to throw new things at us, there is always a reason to laugh at ourselves. Laughter is the main method for remaining oneself. This is why latter-day Kazakh millionnaires are happy to tell jokes about themselves, believing in their souls that they are actually still the same unselfish lads they once were. Those around them are content for them to remain under this naïve delusion.

SOME WORDS ON LOVE AND MARRIAGE

The traditional Kazakh epos left us many fabulous monuments of the poetic art and in each work of popular folklore we find the subject revolves around love. The epic heroes perform great deeds, save the motherland, destroy huge armies of enemies, but all this is but a background for the amorous theme. Here, the Kazakhs did not go far from the plot lines that are common around the world. In the end it all comes down to a simple formula: boy meets girl; boy loses girl; boy finds girl.

Although the majority of tales end happily ever after, there are also poems of a tragic nature. In their scale they are comparable to the best examples of world literature, achieving true passion on a Shakespearian scale. History has concealed the names of the authors of these fabulous epic poems, but it can be assumed that these were creators of a Homeric level. Military scenes are intertwined with love dramas, among which the heroes are Kazakh Romeos and Juliettes, Tristans and Isoldes, Lancelots and Guineveres. The heroes of these epics act, they are victorious and sometimes they die in the name of their loved ones.

It should be noted that unlike the male characters that amaze the listener with their power, incredible strength, muscular torsos, wondrous flying horses, magic swords and the like, the female characters are distinguished by their intelligence, active nature, keen wit and resourcefulness. They are more realistic and, therefore, they are more attractive. All of these qualities are used for one objective alone: to ease the path of the sweetheart to her heart and then to the wedding feast. The description of the latter event occupies a vast finale for any epos. The listener is bombarded with descriptions of how many herds of sheep and horses were eaten at the wedding feast; how many rivers of mares' milk were drunk. Here it is assumed, which goes without saying, that the bride is the epitome of earthly beauty, while her groom is incredibly strong and powerful. The most common comparison for female beauty is the orb of night, the moon. The moon for the Kazakhs is a symbol of femininity and everything beautiful. Therefore, traditional women's names in Kazakh are full of components which include the word Selena, or Ai in Kazakh (for example, Aigul, meaning moonflower or Ainur, meaning moonlight and so on).

In this way, from their youth, the Kazakhs grew up on amorous lyrics, although the real life of the nomads was not particularly synonymous with gracefulness. So, how did this nation manage in real life to combine love in its lofty and delicate manifestations with the harsh life of the steppe nomads? To be honest, we have no answer to the question. Judging by the fact that we are still alive and fairly numerous, it appears the Kazakhs somehow resolved the problem.

Fragmentary descriptions in fictional literature, the sketches of ethnographers and the tales of our grandmothers help us to build a picture. Love games and amusements of the young appear mostly in the warmer months of the year in spring and summer. After the Kazakhs completed the celebration of the great festival of Nauryz, the festival of spring and the vernal solstice which symbolizes the start of a new life, games were played at night in the auls using bones. A snow-white bone was thrown into the darkness and couples would rush out into the aromatic steppe grass to search for it. At times such searches would go on for hours, by which time the couples would presumably have had the opportunity to resolve any serious problems, exchange vows of trust and first kisses.

The autumn was a time for weddings, but before each wedding there came a most important process, the matchmaking. Love was one thing, but the matter involved social and even political interests. Marriage for Kazakhs was a very important institution, securing bonds between clans, ensuring the unity of the nation and its genetic and spiritual kinship. Entering family bonds, each clan needed to give a good account of itself. The groom paid the corresponding kalym, the price for the bride, to the family or the clan from whence the bride hailed. In her turn, she would bring a considerable dowry into the new family, which underscored the wealth of her clan.

After the wedding a totally new life would begin for the bride. The previous ties with her clan were almost completely broken and she and her children became an integral part of the clan she married into. In this way, marriage and family ties firmly cemented the Kazakhs together as a nation.

The status of women in Kazakh society was drastically different from that of the Kazakhs' Islamic neighbours. A Kazakh woman would never cover her face with a yashmak, she would gallop on horseback no worse than a man and with time would take complete control over the holding and the livestock. Accordingly, she would retain real control over the family, allowing the men to decide global political issues.

During the period of modernization in the twentieth century, the role of the Kazakh woman in society underwent a change, but her status as commander-in-chief in the family remained unaltered. This enabled the Kazakhs, alongside strong, close, family ties, to survive in the literal sense of the word over the course of various demographic and social disasters of the tempestuous last century.

However, relationships in the love sense changed dramatically. During the period of communist modernization, Kazakh girls willingly supported a rejection of archaic traditions, were delighted to dress in European clothes and came to behave in a much more uninhibited way with the opposite sex. Indeed, the generation of our parents, whose youth was spent in this time, considered itself very progressive and liberated. On the other hand, our generation, whose youth was spent during the sexual revolution of the 1970s, saw its parents as an object of ridicule and an example of traditional archaicism. Today, we are coming to be viewed in the same way by our own children, who see us as the so-called *Sovoks*,[22] who, by a strange coincidence outlived their own country the Soviet Union.

One way or another, the relationships between young people in the latter half of the twentieth century altered significantly; they became freer and the compulsion to get married disappeared. The kalym transformed into a seldom-encountered and exotic custom. Relationships became simpler, and the traditional system of close family ties was seriously eroded and considerably weakened.

What remained unchanged was the human feeling, the principle of which is love. So, as was the case hundreds of years ago, young hearts tremble at the sight of the subject of their tender affection, whose voice alone can make these hearts miss a beat. In the same way as before, love dramas unfold and young hearts are broken because of unhappy love.

Oh, Moon, guardian of loved ones, please protect our children from an aching heart!

---

[22] 'Sovok' is a derogatory term for a resident of the Soviet Union, deprived of access to the good things from the Western market such as fashionable clothes and the other attributes of a consumer society. This labelling was originally intended to express disdain on the part of the young people, more progressive in terms of getting to know Western civilization, but in time it acquired a somewhat lyrical and gently nostalgic connotation.

3

Geography and Public Life

HOW TO GET AROUND KAZAKHSTAN

It is difficult to speak of a country the size of Western Europe by applying geographic standards that are understood by Europeans. Kazakhstan is a country that is five times the size of France or nine times the size of Germany-at least, as the propaganda of the Soviet age liked to reiterate. Countries that are comparable with Kazakhstan in terms of territory, climate and geography are Canada and Australia.

Indeed, Kazakhstan is somehow comparable with an entire continent, or a giant island, cast into the depths of Eurasia. Its main and central part is comprised of plains and steppes, while its natural borders are the Siberian forests in the north, the Caspian Sea in the west, deserts and the Aral Sea in the south and mountains in the east. You can find many varied landscapes in Kazakhstan, from lush oasis to Martian desert, from alpine meadows to enormous canyons. Naturally, it is no easy matter travelling over such a vast area. Neverthelesss, the entire country is served by an extensive transport and communications network.

The traditional modes of transport, the horse and the camel, have long since made way for other, more contemporary means of travel, yet over small distances on a local scale these creatures continue to be used to great effect as irreplaceable and ecologically-friendly assistants to us humans. Of course, for the tourists wishing to immerse themselves in the romanticism of the steppe, a saddled horse can always be found as also, if one tries, can a camel.

Kazakhstan is rich in fauna, including the bear, wolf and fox. The last tiger was seen back in 1936, in the River Ili floodplain near Lake Balkhash, but it is hoped these beautiful striped predators still reside among the rushes of the great rivers Ili and Syr-Daria.

There are those who hunt bear in the Altai Mountains and wolves just about everywhere. Wolf numbers have risen in recent years to such an extent that their control has now become a state problem. Those fearful about meeting a wolf face to face can always take a helicopter. Arabian princes made it a custom to travel to Kazakhstan to hunt with falcons. This is an ancient and exotic form of hunting but those prepared to equal the money paid by Arab sheikhs are catered for. In the troubled and chaotic times of the 1990s falcon smuggling was a profitable business, but the government gradually managed to put this house in order and these birds now grace the native expanses with their hunting scream, seeking out the fox, wolf or hare, the main prey in hunting with falcons; the larger prey being hunted with golden eagles.

For the fishermen, Kazakhstan boasts charming places for any kind of fishing (excluding the outlawed pastime of fishing with dynamite). A fisherman's dream of catching a half-ton beluga, bursting with tens of kilogrammes of caviar was, until recently, a very achievable goal. The Aral Sea, a pearl in the desert, has become catastrophically shallow and scientists have even described it as history's worst ecological disaster at the hands of humans. In the Caspian Sea the so-called caviar mafia, using the universal disorder that followed the fall of the USSR, brought the sturgeon to almost total extinction and international organizations announced a moratorium on the sale of Caspian caviar. However, in recent years some progress is visible, with Kazakhstan succeeding almost independently, but with some international support, in reviving its part of the Aral Sea, transformed into desert by the economic activity of the Soviets, involving wasteful cotton and other irrigation projects. Fish have now returned to the Aral Sea and soon the noble fish will be accessible to fishermen again. In the Caspian, Russia and Kazakhstan are fighting hard to save the sturgeon and there is hope that the Caspian Sea will return to its former glory as the fishing centre for this part of Eurasia.

But let us return to travel. For the most part Kazakhstan is a country on dry land, but here and there water transport is used, specifically on the Caspian Sea, the Aral Sea and Lake Balkhash. There is also a well-developed network of riverways in the south-east, north-east and northern parts of Kazakhstan. In its time, in its rush for inexpensive electricity, the Soviet Union built huge hydroelectric plants, creating artificial lakes, which then became a favourite leisure and bathing destination for Kazakhstanis. Water transport is not the favourite for the residents of Kazakhstan, and for obvious reasons, but as more and more prosperous people appear in Kazakhstan, yachting is now gaining in popularity. Latter-day yachtsmen are actively mastering their own lakes, Kapchagai (an artificial sea near the former capital Alma-Ata) and Borovoe (an incredibly beautiful, but glacial wonder of nature, not far from the new capital Astana) and the water expanses of their neighbours, particularly Lake Issyk-Kul in neighbouring Kyrgyzia.[1]

From an economic point of view, rail travel is the most important form of transport in Kazakhstan. In its time, the Russian Empire began laying strategic rail routes, linking Central Asia with the mother country through Kazakhstan. This enabled certain politicians on the Thames to cry out about Russia soon to make inroads into India. This is where the myth arose about the Russian threat and the Great Game. The Soviet regime continued to build rail links, joining Siberia with Kazakhstan and other states in Central Asia. The full value of the great Asian railway network was revealed during the Second World War, when all military factories and other industrial infrastructure had to be evacuated from the European part of the country, while a huge volume of military equipment and combat forces had to be moved west from the Asian part. The railway today is the most economical and, thus, most popular form of transport for the population.

Furthermore, the bulk of goods and freight for export and import within the country is still carried by rail. The rail network is an important part of various projects in a series involved in resurrecting the Great Silk Road between Asia and Europe. As a rule, all these projects and their variations cross the territory of Kazakhstan. Some experts are sure that there are potential advantages in transporting goods from East Asia to Western Europe over land compared with transport by sea. There could be gains both in time and cost. Therefore, the Kazakhstani railways could

---

[1] Under an irony of fate, this is the nearest major expanse of water to the southern capital Alma-Ata, yet it is screened off by a chain of mountains. In Soviet times Issyk-Kul was the favourite resort for residents of Alma-Ata and they considered it their own. The emergence of sovereign states put an end to the habits of considering everything for common use. Kazakhstan is now endeavouring, with new economic means, to 'return' this lake, one of the most beautiful in the world, back under its control.

become an important part of the global economy. There is just one thing to consider when shipping freight from Shanghai to Rotterdam through the middle of Asia and that is the minor detail of the difference in the track gauge: unlike other countries, where the European continental standard has been adopted, the former USSR used a slightly wider gauge. Back then this difference did not stop the Germans in their eastern advances and they learned to overcome the problem with ease. Today, however, when we are talking about the fate of a global project, everything is put in doubt because of the capricious nature of some unknown offcial who, in the middle of the nineteenth century, introduced a track gauge that differed from the European standard.

Road transport is a new element for major transport projects of geo-economic significance. In recent years it has become of strategic importance for Kazakhstan. While the roads in this country leave much to be desired, the government (sometimes with the help of international grants) is maintaining an active policy in the reconstruction of old and the building of new, state-of-the-art motorways. Perhaps it will be the road routes and not the railways, the construction of which would require enormous investment, that will take on the role of the new Silk Road.

We should add that as the citizens of Kazakhstan experience economic growth and improved prosperity, the car has become a widespread phenomenon. The automobile pool is currently growing at a rapid pace and Kazakhstan is encountering problems the likes of which it has not seen before: heavy traffic and jams on the streets, environmental pollution, insufficient parking spaces, etc. These problems first appeared in the country's major cities, but they are gradually encompassing other cities too.

Another strategically important mode of transport is aviation. This makes sense considering the size of Kazakhstan and it is also of primary importance for links with the outside world. All important capital cities lie far to the west: Moscow by air takes four hours, Frankfurt, Amsterdam and London take seven, Istanbul and Beijing take five. However, it was suddenly revealed that the nearest capitals of major powers to Alma-Ata (the republic's principal air gateway) are New Delhi (three and a half hours), Islamabad (two hours) and Kabul (an hour and a half), although this is not a favoured destination.

All of Kazakhstan's major cities and the two capitals are linked by air routes, served by large, modern airliners, while the regional centres are connected with the provincial towns by small aircraft, reminiscent of the 1920s and 1930s. The people call them crop-dusters, as this type of aircraft was used in Soviet times to spray fertilizer and insecticides over crops, occasionally over plants and also for irrigation. It should be remembered that the agricultural areas of certain major farms in Kazakhstan can be the size of some European countries.

Previously, helicopters were the exclusive province of the military and academics, but in recent years private choppers have appeared too. They are used mostly to travel around those regions with a complex geography and mountainous landscape. Tourists also have the chance to travel by helicopter to visit the wonderful nature parks, hidden high in the mountains. Helicopters are also an irreplaceable aide when it comes to searching for cosmonauts. Yes, Kazakhstan has another mode of transport possessed by a handful of world powers – spacecraft.

After the fall of the Soviet Union, Kazakhstan was left with the enormous Baikonur Cosmodrome, the area of which exceeds the territory of the Benelux countries put together. This truly giant complex, the offspring of the Soviet rocket and space programme, ensured Soviet supremacy in this field for a considerable time. It was from here that the first human in space lifted off. For many long decades, any information linked with this project was held in the strictest secrecy. Today, though, all who wish may visit the Cosmodrome and admire the unforgettable spectacle of the launch of the latest rocket into Earth's orbit.

Baikonur is the property of Kazakhstan, although Russia leases it for its own use. Russia and Kazakhstan jointly undertake a number of space projects and launch satellites. The crews of spacecraft have included several Kazakhs and new teams are now being prepared, to include Kazakh pilots and scientists. A truly original idea of the Russian directors of the space programme was to launch so-called 'space tourists' into orbit, who are given the opportunity to live for ten days with the crew of the International Space Station. Such a trip costs from 20 to 25 million dollars with a preparation period of between one and two years. So, if you have the air fare and the desire for space travel, Kazakhstan is able to offer you the opportunity.

The cities of Kazakhstan have a variety of public transport systems: buses, trolleybuses and trams, but no underground rail system. In Soviet times, only major cities with a population of over one million had the right to have a metro system built. When the capital of Soviet Kazakhstan Alma-Ata reached this level (in 1981) the question was raised about the construction of an underground. This was also required as a matter of prestige; Tashkent, the capital of competing Soviet republic Uzbekistan, already had its own metro.[2] However, from the mid-1970s, another project has been under discussion: the construction of a high speed rail link on a magnetic cushion (similar to the JR-Maglev by Japan Railways Group). At that time the USSR had similar technologies and was far ahead of West Germany and Japan. It was Alma-Ata that was to become, by 1980, the first city in the Soviet Union with a high-speed link. As a result of intrigues among party officials, the super-modern project for the magnetic link was buried and in the last years of the Soviet Union Alma-Ata saw the start of the construction of an underground system, which still remains unfinished.

The southern capital has another form of transport that is for many unusual – cable-car. But we have already moved into the subject of the next section.

ONE CAPITAL IN THE SOUTH . . .

If there were to be a competition for the country with the most capital cities, then Kazakhstan should surely be crowned champion. In its centuries-old history this country has changed its capital a dozen times. We will not speak of the glory days of the huge nomadic empires, with their headquarters spread across a giant territory within Eurasia to astound their contemporaries. Let us stick with the Kazakh Khanate. The traditional centre, shrine and place where the deceased khans were buried was the city of Turkestan (its ancient name was Yasi) with its wonderful Mausoleum of Khoja Ahmed Yasawi. All the Kazakh khans are buried not far from this grand structure, which was built by the great Timur in honour

---

[2] Tashkent was devastated by an earthquake in 1966. All the efforts of the USSR were directed at rebuilding the Uzbek capital. As a result of the reconstruction and modernization, Tashkent acquired an underground rail network, which serves mostly a decorative function. However, Alma-Ata, which is also under the constant threat of an earthquake, preferred not to build an underground at such a price.

of the glorified Sufi mystic and philosopher. This was a kind of steppe version of the tomb of St Denis, near Paris.

Turkestan remained the official capital for the Kazakh tribes but as the unified state became more fragmented, the leader of each horde established his own headquarters. After Kazakhstan was joined with Russia, the country found itself divided in an administrative sense into two parts. One was controlled from Orenburg in Siberia, the other from Tashkent in Central Asia. Therefore, after the Revolution in 1917, when the Kazakhs were able to form their own state for a short period of time, they found they had two capitals at the same time: Orenburg as the centre of the new state, Alash-Orda[3] and Tashkent, the capital of the Kokand autonomy. The truth is that the Kazakhs were forced to share the capital with their neighbours the Uzbeks, the Kyrgyzis and the Tajiks. After the formation of the USSR, Orenburg remained a part of Soviet Russia, while Tashkent, at the time populated predominantly by Kazakhs, went to the Uzbeks.

Thus, the Kazakhs remained without a capital city. At first, its role was filled by the small town of Kzyl-Orda, earlier bearing the name Perovsk.[4] However, the leaders of the new regime were fed up with living in the desert and they managed to obtain Moscow's permission to move the capital to the city of Verny,[5] which shortly before this acquired its historical name of Alma-Ata (Father-Apple, or Yablochnoe). And they did not regret it. Alma-Ata lay as if in a bowl, surrounded on all sides by a chain of majestic mountains and only accessible from the north. The climate in these places, known from ancient times as Semirechie, was moderate and in Alma-Ata itself – close to European. In the morning a light breeze would blow down from the hills, filling the city with a fresh alpine aroma.

---

[3] The young state received this name in honour of the legendary forefather of all Kazakhs, Alash.

[4] Named so in honour of the Russian general who, in the nineteenth century, headed the progression of the Russian frontier to the south-east. The historical name of this place was Ak-Mechet, meaning 'white mosque'. Anyone who visits this place will understand where the name came from; the blinding sun makes everything seem white, not just the mosque.

[5] Verny (The Loyal). The Russians gave this name to their most south-easterly outpost in Central Asia, created as a counterbalance to the Chinese and the British.

In the spring the main component of these aromas was the fragrance of apple blossom. Apple trees grew both around and within the city itself in huge numbers and this is why it was given its name – the Father-Apple. Marco Polo and John de Plano Carpini noted this fact when they travelled through these parts to Mongolia and China and they described them in their travel notes, labelling this settlement as Yablochnoe (Almalyk). However, historians argue about the precise location of Yablochnoe and some are inclined to move it 20–30 kilometres to the west along the Great Silk Road.

The appearance of a small fortification in the foothills of Ala-Tau, which soon became a town, was an act of geopolitical significance. The Russian Empire was asserting itself in Turkestan in earnest and for the long term: Verny was to show to the Qing and the British the limits of their penetration into Central Asia. Initially, the entire population of the fortification consisted of 470 people. When the fort began to expand, it was built on the principle of an ancient Roman military camp, with the plan being strictly right-angled; this has been retained to this day. By 1867, the population had already reached 10,000 and the fortress obtained the status of a city. Workers and landless peasants came to settle in Verny (most of whom arrived illegally), and Cossacks were sent here under an organized programme.

From the very beginning Verny developed as a political settlement. This melting pot contained a mix of Kazakhs, Russians, Uzbeks and Tatars, Uygurs and Dungans, Jews and Germans. The trade and economic significance of this major centre in Semirechie grew quickly but nevertheless Verny held a strategic military and political significance for the empire. The political factor will always play a primary role in the history of Alma-Ata; based on political considerations it was made the capital of Kazakhstan and based on political considerations it was deprived of the status of a capital city.

In 1905, Verny had a population of 26,000: they were serviced by just fifteen hired *brichkas* (horse-drawn carriages). Clearly the problem of gridlock was not quite as acute then as it is now. The first automobile at this time was brought in by the Russo-Chinese Bank in 1911. It should be said that, in the early twentieth century, Verny was not only a city of soldiers, merchants and gardeners (by this time the fame of the Semirechie apples had already resounded around the country). There were people living here who reached for the skies. Some of them fought in France as aviators during the First World War.[6]

In the spring of 1918, the residents of Verny suddenly found themselves in the Soviet era: in the city a group of opportunists proclaimed Soviet power. The city had to swallow the evils of civil war and political repression (the famous Kazak uprising, described by the revolutionary writer Furmanov), but not as bad as other Siberian and Turkestani cities. On the whole Verny (Alma-Ata from 1921) remained much as it had been: a quiet, provincial little city, cut off from the outside world by mountains and steppe land. Its fate took a dramatic turn in 1928 with the completion of the construction of the Turksib (the Turkestan to Siberia railway – another strategic military and geopolitical moment in Kazkhstan's history) and, in connection with this, the capital of the Kazakh Soviet Republic was moved from the hot Kzyl-Orda to the cool Alma-Ata.

From then until the present day, the city has been growing dynamically and constantly: when the capital was moved there, Alma-Ata had a population of 45,000 people; in 1933, there were 168,000; in 1938, – 270,000; in 1966, – 600,000; in 1981 – a million. No one knows for sure what the exact population is now, but the city draws in its population like a sponge and the figure is no less than a million and a half. However, we shall return to the past. The tram era in Alma-Ata began in 1936 with ten trams serving a twelve-kilometre line. This mode of transport remained the principal way of getting about the city for several decades. Today, however the San Francisco example, it has only been possible to preserve a small section of the tramlines. The capital of Soviet Kazakhstan took shape like a Central Asian urban phenomenon, during the 'golden' years of the Brezhnev-Kunaev era which lasted from the 1950s to the 1970s.

The generation that is now creating the new state and which controls an independent Kazakhstan is comprised of the 'children of the stagnation', i.e. the people who grew up in this period. The vast majority of these people are either citizens of Alma-Ata, or

[6] During the Battle of Verdun, a period that was critical for the Entente, Russia, itself choked by the force of the German armies, sent its detachments to help the allies on the Western Front.

people who were educated in Alma-Ata at that time. It would not be an exaggeration to say that in that era, in the 1960s and 1970s, the character of the city's residents was formed: a mix of refinement and opportunism, finesse and disorder, chumminess and snobbism, internationalism and brotherhood. For the young, Alma-Ata was a city of joy, love and youth, open to the sun, the mountains and the fresh air and imbued with clear light.

In the 1960s and 1970s a kind of sub-culture took shape, brought about by the youth and, primarily, by the students. Many from this sub-culture had features that were common with the youth culture of other Central Asian capitals and generally of the major Soviet cities, but there was something else, something difficult to pinpoint, which made those from Alma-Ata different from the rest and which interrelated them and helped them be recognized in other republics, in Moscow and then abroad as well. During the spring and summer evenings, when the air in the centre of the city becomes soft and full of the aromas from the foothills of Ala-Tau, the lanes and squares would fill with young people and the place would come alive on the benches beneath the canopy of the trees; the strumming of guitars would accompany songs about love, friendship and brotherhood, eternal and beautiful.

A major element of Alma-Ata's sub-culture were the restaurants where many rock groups could hone their skills; playing music in restaurants enabled many amateur groups to make ends meet. In this sub-culture all the hopes and ideals of the youth of the time were sublimated in concentrated form: anti-war emotions and a calling for peace, brotherhood and love. In this way, Alma-Ata at that time was reminiscent of Liverpool in the 1960s. There was another important component of life and the sub-culture of Alma-Ata, where ensembles and music played an important role, and that was Issyk-Kul. As the high society of Paris and other European capitals would head out to the summer resort zones, so the Alma-Ata youth, from late June to early September would be drawn to the banks of what they saw as the clearest and most beautiful lake in the world.

The early 1990s were not the best years for Alma-Ata. The whims of history and the will of others hit the city hard. It came to be like a Balzac coquette, where the features of a beauty that once was could barely be seen through her layer of make-up. The city's buildings, not yet old, looked as though they had darkened and turned grey. The green covering, under which so many comedies, dramas and adventures were once played out, was disappearing. The money-grabbing and excessive commercial trading had spoilt not only the city landscape, but the souls of the people themselves. The wind of change and the walk of life took the residents of Alma-Ata in many different directions; some swapped their jeans for the smart suit of an Astana official, while others found themselves in a different country altogether.

It is simply a miracle that Alma-Ata got through these years. In 1993, a decision was made to name the city in just the Kazakh version – Almaty.[7] In 1994, parliament made a decision to move the capital of Kazakhstan to the Virgin Lands in the steppe and from 1997 this process began. Almaty was unofficially given the honorary but meaningless name of 'Southern Capital'. This euphemism was to conceal the painful loss of the status of capital but, in reality, Almaty remains the genuine capital and favourite city for the majority of Kazakhstanis and especially for those of its sons who, thanks to the will of destiny, found themselves some thousand kilometres further north. As a rule they see their time in the new capital as a protracted business trip. Perhaps in a generation the situation will change. However, as before, the city by the snowy mountain ridges will beckon and draw more and more new romantics.

At the end of the 1990s, and at the start of this century, a sea change took place and the city found itself actively under construction. Almaty was seeing the same process as occurred with Moscow five years earlier, only on a smaller scale. The city grew beautiful again, but this was now the beauty of a mature woman. Many pompous buildings and monumental structures appeared. Almaty adopted something from Istanbul (at the initial stage the reconstruction actively involved Turks, who, accordingly, imposed their own aesthetic tastes) and something from post-Soviet Moscow with its pseudo-Gothic and quasi-European style. However, the centre of the city retains its charm. You can see this for yourself by visiting what is one of the most beautiful cities in Eurasia.

---

[7] Other countries are faced with the same situation: Indians are trying to get the world to call Bombay Mumbai and the Chinese want Peking to be called Beijing, and they are helped in this by the UN.

. . . AND ONE CAPITAL IN THE NORTH

Kazakhstan's capital is now called Astana. This is the literal translation from Kazakh for *capital*.[8] In 1994, the Kazakhstani parliament (at the time it was still known by its Soviet name – Supreme Soviet) voted to move the capital of the young independent state from Almaty to another city, which was then called Akmola. In 1997, the process of creating the new capital began.

The city of Akmola was founded in 1830 by the Russian army as a fortress. A site was selected for a military fortification, determined by its strategic position: it facilitated control over the principal transport and communication links in the region, both overland and by river. However, because of the climate the location was not altogether suitable for habitation. Future residents of Astana were to remember the founders of the city with 'kind' words. From 1832, the city bore the name Akmolinsk, somewhat adapted to the Russian language (in Kazakh it was Akmola or Akmoly). For a century and a half the town was a sleepy, provincial place, coming to life only during the time of the seasonal fairs.

In the 1950s and 1960s, the city attracted universal attention during the famous and, at the same time, somewhat adventurous campaign initiated by the Soviet leader Nikita Khrushchev concerning the development of the so-called Virgin Lands. This is how Kazakhstan got its own Virginia (for those who have forgotten, one of the regions in the south was called Texas). The city, renamed Tselinograd in 1961 (meaning the capital of the Virgin Lands) became the centre of this new, enormous region, designated for the mass production of wheat. But Khrushchev's plans went further than that. As we know, as a result of the mass colonization and deportation, industrial and agrarian migration, northern and central Kazakhstan found itself settled predominantly by expatriates from European Russia; Slavic peoples and Germans. In particular, many Germans settled in the Tselinograd Region. Therefore, on the basis of five regions of Kazakhstan, Khrushchev organized the so-called

---

[8] In connection with this, those who regularly use the Kazakh language find themselves in an awkward situation. To express the meaning of the word 'capital' (when speaking, for example, about other countries) they have to use various new formations and euphemisms with words borrowed from other Eastern languages, classical or ancient-Turkic: 'baskent', 'baskala' and other terms that mean 'the main city'.

Virgin District (Tselinny Krai) with its capital in Tselinograd. A further step was to be the annexing and transfer of this region (a third of the area of the republic and over half of its industrial and agrarian potential) to become a part of Russia.

However, as a result of the overthrow of Khrushchev in 1964 Leonid Brezhnev came to power, who knew Kazakhstan well from the time he had headed the campaign in the 1950s to develop the republic's Virgin Lands. Brezhnev's leadership overturned Khrushchev's administrative innovation and this region, important from every point of view remained a part of Kazakhstan. However, in 1977 came the first threat: the German population, deported by Stalin at the start of the war and resettled to Siberia and North Kazakhstan, started to demand autonomy within the republic. The then leadership of Kazakhstan succeeded in breaking up these separatist plans that threatened the integrity of the republic, as this could have set a precedent for demands for autonomy or secession on the part of the Uygurs in the south-east and the Russians in the north of Kazakhstan.

Events in other regions during the collapse of the Soviet Union displayed the wisdom of the policy to suppress attempts to fragment Kazakhstan on an ethnic basis. On the eve of the collapse of the USSR the city received back its historical name of Akmola, but in 1998, when it had already officially fulfilled the function of capital city for a year, Akmola was renamed Astana.[9] In reality, the city was really only able to fulfil the functions of a capital in the millennium year of 2000, when the majority of the ministries had moved to the northern city.

At the time there was much conjecture as to why Nursultan Nazarbaev decided to move the capital from the beautiful and warm city in the south to the harsh environment in the north. Here are several of the most popular versions. The first was seismic or ecological and seismic. Almaty is indeed located in a dangerous seismic region and maintaining the functions of a capital city in the face of a serious earthquake could not be guaranteed.[10] From

[9] It is generally thought that this renaming was brought about because of the unsavoury sounding name: Akmola translated from Kazakh could have the meaning 'white grave' although idiomatically it most likely meant 'an abundance of white'.

[10] As if the destruction (Heaven forbid!) of Almaty without its capital-city status would not be a catastrophe for all of Kazakhstan!

an ecological point of view, and, unfortunately, this is not that far from the truth: Almaty is at overload, there is no breathing space and ecologically it is nearing critical level.

The second version is 'Chinese'. In the early 1990s there was great concern that China was on the verge of swallowing up 'defenceless Kazakhstan' (some hotheads even called for not handing over nuclear weapons to Russia). The move of the capital far to the north would apparently reinforce the security of the young state.[11]

The third version is 'Russian'; it also comes from the realm of conspiracy theory, it is the direct opposite of the 'Chinese' version and it is also connected with security. According to this point of view, experiencing pressure from the local Russian population, which had been striving, it seemed, to reunite with its historical homeland, Kazakhstan resolved to move the capital to a region, populated predominantly by a Russian-speaking population, to strengthen control on the part of the new Kazakh leadership and the subsequent Kazakhization of the northern regions.

The fourth version is 'economic' and is just as inoffensive as the first. It assigns exclusively economic and administrative motives for the move. Astana is situated in the centre of the country, so it is considerably easier to manage the republic as a whole as well as its individual districts from this point. Furthermore, the development of Astana will push economic growth, both in the new capital and in neighbouring regions; it will strengthen economic and transport links between all administrative and economic districts of Kazakhstan. Strictly speaking, this is precisely what has happened.

Finally, there is the 'internal' version, which is purely related to domestic policy. According to some, the president of the young country decided to break away from the influence of traditional clans, which was particularly prevalent in the south of the republic, and untie its hands in its domestic policy, unite the interests of all regional groups on the basis of a new concensus and commence the construction of a new Kazakhstan, so to speak, from scratch.

None of these versions stands up to criticism if taken individually, but together they give grounds for an additional, although not

[11] As if anyone or anything could stop China if it decided to embark on such a step!

decisive, argument. This, though, was not the most important thing. This was quickly understood by those powers abroad who welcomed any step by Kazakhstan away from the Soviet past and movement towards an independent state with a new identity. In this way, the move of the capital was primarily a step in the direction of creating and securing a new national identity and nothing other than that. Astana was to symbolize the creation of a new Kazakhstan which was to be almost completely unconnected with its Soviet past, although the modern Kazakh state was actually formed on a Soviet foundation. However, in years to come as the generations change, who will remember that there was once a Kazakh Soviet Socialist Republic with its capital city in Alma-Ata?

As history shows, Kazakhstan was not the first to make this choice. China and Japan in Asia, Spain and Russia in Europe and more recently Brazil and Malaysia have all moved their capital cities. The reasons and the results of these political gestures were different in each case, but the main reason was to assert a new political reality in the form of a new regime, a new identity and a new symbol. In Russia there was a return to the past: in 1918, the communists returned to Moscow the status of the official centre of an enormous Eurasian power (as St Petersburg symbolized the 'European' aspect of Russia's development).[12]

But let us return to the recent moves of capitals. It was at this time (1998–99) that the new German government of Social-Democrats and the Greens changed the location of the capital's ministries, moving them from the banks of the Rhine to the Spree. The return to Berlin, against which many West Germans who had grown up in Bonn objected, had the same objective as in Kazakhstan – the underscoring of one's national identity and historical succession. However, some were inclined to think that they were seeing a return to a Prussian tradition or a Reich tradition, which Berlin had once symbolized. But as a result something quite

[12] The example of Russia has a particular significance for Kazakhstan. It is considered that Kazakhstan is repeating its path but, taking account of Russia having ten times the magnitude, all parameters for Kazakhstan are presented in a form that is ten times smaller. This means, for example, that if Russia returned its capital to Moscow after 200 years, Kazakhstan should do this in about twenty, i.e. in about 2017–19.

different began to form: a Berlin Republic, uniting within itself features of West and East Germany.[13]

And there is something similar happening in Kazakhstan as well. If the capital city had remained in Almaty we would most likely be seeing a continuation of former traditions, retained by the former elite, based in the south and thinking with a Soviet mind-set. However, the move of the capital yielded a surprising result, which is clearly what the authors of the project were counting on. Astana became the centre for the formation of a new Kazakhstani idenitity, more than Kazakh, more than Soviet, more than Russian, more than regional and more than clan-based. That said, the former differences between residents are still retained to a great extent.

The move of the capital in Kazakhstan at the turn of the century occurred with a truly epic flourish and it was accompanied with dramas in the true style of old. If the German bureaucrats shuddered at the thought of having to leave their cosy offices on the Kennedy Allee or the Rheinufer and move to the gloomy, grey, Prussian and post-communist Berlin, the Almaty officials felt much the same. Nevertheless, in one instance it was German discipline, in the other the iron will of Kazakhstan's leader that brought both these countries to one and the same result. Both Berlin and Astana in these years were typical construction landscapes with tall cranes creating a similar backdrop.

The officials moaned and groaned but they soon grew accustomed to the new conditions. An important fact should be pointed out here, which distinguished the situation in Kazakhstan from that in Germany. Unlike the German bureaucrats who left Bonn for the well-organized Berlin, the Kazakh officials moved to a small provincial town, where the infrastructure left much to be desired. Refined bureaucrats were housed several to a hostel room,

---

[13] The following aspect also generates parallels with the situation around the return of the German capital to Berlin: the typical person travelling almost daily and certainly between Tegel and Frankfurt or Cologne/Bonn was the bureaucrat or financial official (especially after the major banks of West Germany moved their headquarters). The new Berliners preferred to spend their weekends on the banks of the Rhine, where they still had their apartments and familiar surroundings. And so likewise in Kazakhstan, where the most frequent flyers between Astana and Alma-Ata are officials, torn between work in the new capital and their families, comforts, relatives and friends in the old.

forcing them to recall their distant student past with its disorderly, basic way of life. Similar conditions awaited them at the workplace, as there were simply no regular, modern offices available. On the whole this was all reminiscent of the development of the Virgin Lands in the 1950s, so the officials were compared with the pioneers of that time. However, unlike the situation during the Soviet period, no one planned to raise monuments or name highways in their honour.

Linked with a certain comic element to this situation, although in reality it was incredibly dramatic (the customary way of life for thousands of people had completely changed overnight), many jokes appeared, often prompted by real-life situations. Thus, it was customary to believe that moving from Almaty to Astana meant passing through four phases. The first was Implantation. The immigrant was introduced to an alien and hostile environment and it was a question of time to see how this southern flower would take to the harsh northern soil. If the implantation look place more or less successfully, the next phase would ensue, known as the 'Alcoholization'. In this instance, no explanation is required. In congested living conditions in a hostel or in an apartment block (when a ministry received its housing quota, all employees were moved into one building) a group of lonely men, away from other forms of entertainment (at first it was the men that headed for Astana) did not take long to remember their student ways and Soviet habits, principally spending time together over a bottle of vodka. In time this became their favourite pastime.

The third phase, which had fatal consequences for many families, was the so-called 'Tokalization'.[14] Alas, during the early period of development of the new capital, all forced settlers arrived without their families. This living apart could drag on for years and was not always the fault of the government. In time all officials were given their own apartments, but their wives and families did not rush to leave their native Almaty. Moreover, many officials were accustomed to spend each weekend in the old capital, if finances would allow. For many years Astana was a ghost town on a Friday night, with everyone rushing to the railway station and the airport to get to Almaty. On Sunday evening or Monday morning a

[14] This flippant term comes from the Kazakh word 'tokal', meaning young (new) wife or, in this case, lover or girlfriend.

similar phenomenon could be observed, only in reverse, from Almaty to Astana. And so it continued until the infuriated president ordered the officials to spend more time in the new capital.

Returning to the question of Tokalization, without lawful wives and left to their own devices, the young and the very young men in Astana gradually found themselves sympathetic female hearts, prepared to smooth over their lonely existence. In time and as happens the world over, these ladies, deeply attached to their chosen ones, began to lay claim to official status. This is how families were destroyed and new ones created, symbolizing not only the power of love but also a new state identity, only in a family context. Not everyone went along with this idea of creating a new family (sometimes in parallel with the original Almaty family), but there can be no doubt that this phenomenon was very widespread. Vigilant wives succeeded in returning some to the bosom of the family or the return of the lost sheep back home, or they moved to the new capital themselves, thus bringing to an end the free-roaming life of these individuals.

Here we naturally arrive at the fourth and final phase of the modern Kazakhstan epic – the 'Evacuation'. This word speaks for itself and means the forced and sometimes hurried return of an individual to Almaty as a consequence of the influence of the second or the third factor and at times of both factors simultaneously. In the majority of cases this automatically signified the end of a career which, for a genuine bureaucrat is a fate worse than death. However, as a result, Astana performed a rare socio-historical experiment in the creation of a breed of officials who were steadfast in the face of deprivation and loyal to a single idea. Once they had passed through the principal phases, the bureaucrats could be used confidently in any circumstances, including expeditions to the Himalayas or the Antarctic. In terms of the staff of the Ministry of Foreign Affairs, for example, this meant that these people could work in any conditions, from Mongolia to the Sahara.

Initially, the newly-arrived Astana residents naturally evoked a whole range of feelings among the old residents with their presence and their behaviour. These feelings were pity (for the southerners who were unaccustomed to the truly Siberian local winters), mockery (look, someone's got blown over by the wind; must be someone from Almaty), irritation (they don't understand the local rules and they just want too much) and hatred (their arrival brought about astronomical price rises on absolutely everything, from housing to local produce). For their part, yesterday's Almaty residents laughed and joked to their heart's content about the provincial locals who to them were like backward residents of Tselinograd. A cause for mockery could be the lack of normal service in restaurants and shops, to which the Almaty residents were able to become accustomed over the years of market reforms, along with the local dialect, mannerisms and customs.

In this way, there were very few situations where these two groups of people, who grew up in the Soviet era, only in completely different conditions, could find any common ground. However, with time, the unthinkable began to happen. As the former Almaty residents grew up and had children of their own in Astana and the city was occupied by migrants from other regions of Kazakhstan, signs appeared of a new capital-city community. These young people saw themselves not as Almaty residents, not Akmola residents; not southerners or northerners, but fully-fledged residents of the new capital and citizens of a new Kazakhstan. The entire might of state propaganda worked flat out to generate this new sense of solidarity.

From the early twenty-first century the new capital of Kazakhstan has come to grow and develop at a very fast pace. By 2005, Kazakhstan's President Nazarbaev could already proudly show Russian leader Vladimir Putin an almost completely new city. But things did not stop there. The tempo of the construction is simply amazing: eyewitnesses and foreign observers are as one when they assert that the new capital is as if rejuvenated every six months. It appears that such rates will be maintained at least until the year 2010. However, even today it is obvious that Astana has for the most part fulfilled its role in forming a new identity for Kazakhstan. Kazakhstan's foreign partners understand this as well. Almost all the embassies have already moved from Almaty to Astana. The first to make the long journey were the embassies of the countries of the CIS, thus demonstrating a solidarity with the Kazakhstan President's grand project. Diplomats from these countries went through the same trials as the Kazakhstan officials themselves. Western embassies dragged their heels for a long time but over a ten-year period they have now built themselves comfortable residences.

Of course, the two capitals continue to compete with one another behind the scenes, but no longer in the way they did before. This is to a great extent thanks to the fact that the former Almaty residents have grown accustomed to life in the new capital, where they often have better and more modern apartments and where their salary is significantly higher than before; for many the opportunity has triggered the prospect of a brilliant career. Their children do not remember Almaty and consider themselves residents of Astana. The customary way of life has changed, as have the former notions and habits. There can be no doubt that in future Astana will play a prominent role in the fate of Kazakhstan and this process has actually already begun. At least no one can any longer refute its role in creating a new identity for Kazakhstan and breaking away from the Soviet past, a symbol of which (perhaps deservedly so) is seen by many as being the once resplendent Almaty.

So, choosing for itself a new capital, Kazakhstan has set out on an unknown yet promising future.

PLACES TO SEE AND THINGS TO DO

It is hard to speak of particular places to see in Kazakhstan, as this is a country that is wholly unknown to foreigners and at the same time it is also immense (not all Kazakhstanis know their motherland in all its geographical and climatic diversity). This would be the same if you were recommended a visit to America or Brazil. The difference is that these two enormous countries are well known to the public, while Kazakhstan is only just opening up to the outside world.

We have already spoken of the geographical diversity of this country. It is true to say that you can find anything here: baking deserts and limitless steppes, prairies that know no end and blossoming oases, peaks that prop up the sky and seas as blue as the sky, mountain torrents and gentle backwater streams. Eco-tourism is only just taking off in Kazakhstan but world experts are as one in the opinion that the prospects are nothing short of fabulous.

The situation with historical monuments is somewhat different. As noted above, Kazakhstan has an incredibly fluid history, which determined that the Kazakhs and their nomadic ancestors gave preference to oral monuments over those of the material kind. Nevertheless, this is far from being a desert in terms of cultural monuments. For thousands of years, the territory of Kazakhstan was a crossroads, where different civilizations and cultures came together, without denying and without destroying, only supplementing, enriching and sequentially replacing one another.

As regards monuments, those worth noting first are the stone sculptures in the form of silent figures, spread over the endless expanses of the Great Steppe. It is possible that they hold someone's secrets; perhaps they are reference points, guarding the route of the wanderers, the dust of which was scattered thousands of years ago. These are the most ancient monuments of material culture within Kazakhstan, if one discounts the relics of the ancient-archaeological age. The burial mounds, dispersed across the steppes are reminiscent of the age of the so-called early nomads, proud warriors who once stopped the phalanxes of Alexander the Great, who had tried to conquer lands to the north of the Ox (now Amu-Daria).[15] There is other mysterious evidence of ancient cultures: the catacombs in the deserts of West Kazakhstan (on the Mangyshlak Peninsula), decorated with astonishing examples of wall paintings dating back to the age of the ancient hunters and nomads. They are no less significant than the famous Pyrenean Caves and, thanks to their cosmogenic nature they really have no equal.

Evidence can even be found of ancient and Hellenistic periods in Kazakhstan; likewise, there are fragments of ancient and medieval China. As far as the Buddhist Age is concerned, which had such a major impact on Central Asia, the region of south and south-east Kazakhstan was an area used by pilgrims, striving to reach India from Eastern Asia and also in reverse: missionaries, bearing the teachings of Prince Gautama to China. The most grandiose monument of that era is the enormous treble image of Buddha, carved into a rocky crag, suspended over the measured flow of the River Ili.[16]

However, for understandable reasons, there are more monuments from the Muslim age in Kazakhstan than any other. And this is easily explained. Islam came to the territory of Kazakhstan in the

---

[15] The most famous find of this kind is the Golden Man. This is a completely intact ceremonial costume made of gold, belonging to a representative of the Saka aristocracy or even to the regal family. This and other finds are on display in the museums of Almaty and Astana.

[16] This miracle of decorative art is only one hundred kilometres from the centre of Almaty. Unfortunately or, more precisely, fortunately, the majority of of the city's residents have never seen or even have any inkling of the existence of such a grand monument. Therefore, it has every chance of remaining untouched for posterity and for the joy of the Dalai Lama. We note that after the barbarous destruction by the Afghan Taliban of the great double monument to Buddha in Bagram, this image remains as the largest in the world, if we discount the giant structures of more ancient eras in China, Thailand and Burma.

eighth century and it is still a part of the national culture and everyday life. We will consider this in more detail later. The main sights of the Islamic civilization are concentrated in southern Kazakhstan. Stylistically and in terms of architecture they are identical to the monuments of Samarkand, Bukhara, Khiva and Khorezm, the great centres of the Muslim world in the pre-Mongol era. We were very fortunate that it was Kazakhstan that came to be the place where the Mausoleum of Khoja Ahmed Yasawi, the great Sufi poet and mystic, held in esteem by the Great Timur, who ordered the building of the grand mausoleum in his honour in the steppe, near the city of Turkestan. In ancient times this complex served as a spiritual school (a madrassa) for the followers of the great Sufi and, at the same time, the shrine of the Kazakh khans.

In the centre of the complex is a giant *kazan*, or cauldron, revered as something sacred by all Kazakhs, who have seen in it a symbol of the sustenance of the nation. As was customary for all European colonizers of the nineteenth century, the Russians removed the sacred relic, taking the cauldron to St Petersburg, where, for many decades, it decorated the Hermitage, the treasure house of the Russian tsar and emperors. The communist authorities moved this symbol of Kazakh survival into a storeroom of the Hermitage, so as not to rouse religious feeling. It was only after the fall of the Soviet Union that the holy kazan was returned to its rightful place, bringing joy to the enthusiasts of popular culture and religious pilgrims. The latter regularly visit the Yasawi complex, which for the Muslims of Central Asia is classed on a level of a 'second Mecca'. A person who twice completed a pilgrimage to the Mausoleum of Khoja Ahmed Yasawi was deemed the equivalent of a pilgrim who had completed a genuine Hajj to Mecca.

Speaking of the diversity of the monuments of different ages and cultures in Kazakhstan, we cannot overlook the influences of Russian and European architecture. Those with an interest in Russian provincial architecture, whch is so poorly represented today within a mostly European Russia, are recommended to look in the wonderful corners of old Russia, that are preserved in the towns of northern Kazakhstan and in certain places in Almaty (the former Verny). It is clear for all to see from these buildings how paradoxically the European stone style, the Russian tradition of building in wood and the eastern environment all combined, forcing builders to seek new solutions in the conditions of a hot climate and design houses for a new landscape and green expanses. What is gratifying is that this tradition of architectural synthesis was preserved in the Soviet period, too, laying the foundations for an original school of architecture, which harmoniously combined elements of European architecture, both traditional and modern, with the eastern tradition of flat roofs, enclosed courtyards and narrow windows.

However, on the whole, the saying 'seeing is believing' is really appropriate in this instance. It is for this reason that we recommend you visit and see what we describe with your own eyes.

Traditional forms of entertainment and games for Kazakhs, known to us from history, are reminiscent of similar leisure pastimes of many patriarchal peoples. The only and important difference was imposed by the nomadic way of life of the Kazakhs and gave rise to wrestling (*kazaksha kures*), competitive horse-racing (*baiga*), singing contests and others. One popular competition was *kokpar,* in which two teams of players compete to carry a headless goat carcass into a goal. As far as the children are concerned, the favourite game was *asyki,* similar to marbles, *gorodki* or skittles, and bowling, only using small bones from the knees of sheep. The bones would be lined up and they would have to be knocked out with another bone of the same kind (only made heavier with a lead insert). The game of asyki, was still being played up until the 1990s and remains part of the culture today.

Regular children's games in the Soviet era differed little from those described in classical literature, especially in Mark Twain's evergreen *The Adventures of Tom Sawyer.* For many decades the most popular games were war-related (against the fascists) and favourite toys had a clearly military theme. This is evidence of the scar in the national memory and a reminder of the most terrible of national tragedies which was the involvement of Soviet society in the Second World War.

Today, the advent of the computer has totally changed the way of life and the nature of children's entertainment and in this Kazakhstan is no exception. As far as traditional, folklore pastimes for adults are concerned, they are preserved here and there as elements of the national cultural heritage. Accordingly, tourists do have the chance to see these ancient rituals at first hand.

The modernization that took place in the twentieth century brought about radical changes not only in the Kazakhs' way of life, but in the way they spend their leisure time. Kazakh men mastered card games in all their variations and subtleties, but one of the most popular was the 'intellectual' game of preference, a three-player game similar to bridge, euchre and five-hundred. However, poker, vingt-et-un and other games, made famous in certain Western films, also found their way into the Kazakh steppe and distingushed masters of the game appeared on the scene. Legends still circulate about one minister from the Soviet era, who booked an entire rail carriage for a card game, in which he battled it out with other aspiring players for the unofficial title of champion. The carriage trundled across the endless steppe expanses, until the representatives of the upper party and Sovet echelons locked horns at the card table, where whole livelihoods were put at stake; this was incredibly strange, given the official ascetic nature of the Soviet regime.

Kazakhstan also adopted other European pastimes, including billiards, dominoes, draughts and chess, making it no different from other parts of the Soviet Union. Chess played an important part in the lives of the men (and many women). This sport, laying claim to high-intellectual status, was supported by the official ideology and was incredibly popular in its own right. All the representatives of the Soviet intelligentsia played chess, especially from the technical professions and exact sciences. Chess created a special aura and helped to attain a high social status. The almost total monopoly in the world hierarchy as held by the Soviet chess school in the twentieth century confirms the truly national character of the game. However, it was a popular game among ordinary people as well, helping to shorten the long, hard winter evenings for Stalin's exiles, geologists enduring difficult expeditions, train passengers crossing great distances lasting many days, and so on.

Even up until recently one could observe lively groups of people enjoying chess on benches in the parks and in the alleys of Alma-Ata. The current generation, who grew up in the Soviet era, copied the older generation through inertia, but soon the dramatic change in the customary way of life and the advent of new forms of entertainment also had an impact on this sphere of social life. New toys appeared: expensive cars, motor boats and yachts, villas and palaces and, finally, personal aeroplanes and helicopters. The opportunity to relax in European, Asian and tropical resorts was also now available. But the new favourite pastime for the Kazakhs was the favourite game of the Americans, known as making money and doing business.

In this way, over the last fifteen to twenty years today's generation of Kazakhs has been busy building a new economy and, at the same time, creating a livelihood for itself. Of course, each commitment meant there was little time for games and relaxation. Customary pursuits for the Western elite quickly bored those with considerable resources. This stage saw the advent of sobriety, forcing the newly-arrived millionaires to yearn with nostalgia for the simple pastimes of their childhood and youth.

KAZAKHSTAN'S COSMIC TOURIST ATTRACTION: BAIKONUR

Among the subjects of local, republican and USSR subordination - spread across the endless steppes of Soviet Kazakhstan - there was one enterprise that could rightly be called a site of geopolitical significance. This was the world-famous Baikonur Cosmodrome, which was destined to become a symbol of the glory of Soviet space exploration demonstrating the geopolitical might of the USSR. After 1991, however, Baikonur almost became a symbol of decay and degradation.

Today, though, the cosmodrome has two masters-Russia and Kazakhstan-and as before, is a complex system for the launch of spacecraft and ballistic missiles. The Cosmodrome is comprised of nine start complexes with fifteen launch installations, thirty-four technical complexes, three fuelling stations and two aerodromes. The Cosmodrome houses the world's largest oxygen-nitrogen plant. It is from this base, served by space defence forces, that almost all of Russia's very latest military and space objects are launched.

The nine start complexes and fifteen launch installations are designed for the launch of the mother carrier spacecraft Tsiklon, Energiya, Molniya, Soyuz and Rokot. However, Bakonur's greatest value for Russia and world cosmonautics lies in the fact that it is only from this cosmodrome that manned spacecraft and heavy Proton rockets, which account for the majority of commercial starts, can be launched. Furthermore, the Cosmodrome has eleven buildings for assembling rockets and satellites. The Cosmodrome covers an area of 7,717 square kilometres. Over 18 million hectares of land are assigned for the fall of the first stages of the rocket. A total of 80,000 people reside across all sites of the Cosmodrome, one half of which are citizens of Kazakhstan, serving the Cosmodrome and its infrastructure.

Today, it is no secret to anyone that both the Soviet and American space programmes owe much of their success to the German missile legacy. However, after the war, this legacy was rather unfairly distributed, giving the British and the Americans fully-tested rockets, an oxygen plant, fuelling and launch equipment and a team with considerable experience of targeting Britain. Most importantly, though, was the fact that they got the father of the FAU rockets, Wernher von Braun, and his colleagues. All the Soviet Union got was parts of the rockets or, at best, untested models. Of the German specialists, the greatest coup was the chief electronics specialist Helmut Grettrup. Those involved in the events recall how the German specialist agreed to move to the USSR and take part in the Soviet missile programme only after he had been promised that his favourite four horses and two cows, looked after by his wife, would be brought over.

It was not long before the Soviet Union felt considerable strategic military pressure from America. The intelligence forces discovered that as early as 1946 von Braun had made calculations for the American Army for the launch of the A-12 ballistic missile. This two-stage missile was presented to the scientific community in October 1950. However, it was not this factor that was the main stimulus for the Soviet strategic programmes: after Winton Churchill's 'Iron Curtain' speech in Fulton, Missouri, it became clear that we could soon see the start of American bombing. The territory of the USSR was vulnerable to America's strategic aviation, based in Europe, the Middle East and Japan. US spy planes crossed Soviet air space with impunity at high altitude. As a result, all the forces of the Soviet Union were chanelled into developing a nuclear and ballistic missile programme.

As it turned out, the test ground and the springboard for these programmes were to be located in Kazakhstan, involving two critical sites: the Semipalatinsk nuclear test ground (Kurchatov) and the Baikonur Cosmodrome (Leninsk). We have already covered the Soviet nuclear programme, but the fact is that without delivery vehicles, even the most powerful nuclear weapons were useless. And so Baikonur appeared on the map, not a cosmodrome at first, rather a testing ground for the launch of ballistic missiles. The folklore of those years retained the expression 'to take a pop at the little white house', applicable to any training target.

Officially, the construction of the Baikonur Cosmodrome began in the Kzyl-Orda Region of the Kazakh SSR under the resolution of the USSR Council of Ministers in February 1955, 'On the Creation of Research Test Ground No. 5'. However, in reality, the strategic military site was developed several years earlier, while the area allocated for the testing ground, or used for the space programme, lay far away from the Kzyl-Orda Region, encompassing considerable chunks of the Djezkazgan and Karaganda regions. Eyewitnesses recall how Sergei Korolev, leader of the entire Soviet rocket programme, sighed on seeing the latest delegation from Kazakhstan at the Central Committee of the Soviet Union Communist Party: 'Here come the Kazakhs to complain again about how I am taking their land away from them.' Indeed, at the time the overall territory of Baikonur could have been compared with the size of the average European country.

It is obvious that Baikonur was created primarily as a strategic military site. A number of specialists even state that the transformation of the military programme into a peaceful space programme was down to chance or, more precisely, to unsuccessful tests of heavy ballistic missiles. Already in February 1956, the Soviet R-5M rocket was the first in the world to carry a nuclear warhead through space. Having travelled 1,200 km the warhead produced an 80 kilotonne nuclear explosion in the region of the Aral Sea in Kara Kum. The development of the thermonuclear warhead enabled the power of the carried charge to be increased to a megatonne.

At first everything went well: victorious reports flew from Baikonur to Moscow after each new launch. However, on 15 May 1957 the first major accident occurred: the R-7 intercontinental ballistic missile was launched for the first time but at the 98th second the controlled flight was stopped. It was as if some omen hung over the R-7; all subsequent launches of this class of rocket were unsuccessful. And it was here that a brilliant idea came to Koroloev and his team of specialists: it was proposed that a 'seven' series class intercontinental ballistic missile be launched, not with a heavy warhead but with a lighter, 'civilian' equivalent. Simple calculations showed that the assumed speed would enable the object to become an artificial Earth satellite. So, on 4 October 1957 a successful launch of the new lighter missile took place and the term *Sputnik* entered the world's languages. In the USA, geopolitical hysteria started, as the Americans understood that the USSR had learned how to produce intercontinental ballistic missiles and America was no longer invulnerable. And they learned the word Baikonur, too.

Soon, the Soviet rockets got as far as the Moon and they photographed its dark side. In 1959, a morose Wernher von Braun, speaking to American journalists, declared that the USSR had overtaken the USA by some margin and no sum of money would buy back the lost time. However, the history of Baikonur, which became a symbol of Soviet cosmonautics, had its difficult and even tragic moments: failed launches, accidents, explosions and disasters. But in 1959–61 the active search for a possible manned flight into orbit saw a series of successful flights, and it all culminated in Gagarin's famous 'Let's go!'[17] This took place on 12 April 1961, with the launch of the Vostok-class rocket from Baikonur. Soviet cosmonautics owed its triumph to the genius of Korolev and to the fact that of the two programmes, Vostok and Zenit, priority was given to the former.

It should be noted that Korolev was under constant pressure from the military. The designer was already fully occupied with plans for peaceful spaceflight, whereas the generals demanded the implementation of defence projects as the first priority. Concensus was only achieved between the Defence Ministry and OKB-1 (Korolev's research and engineering office) when Korolev combined his rocket programme with the creation of an automatic camera-carrying satellite. This is how the Zenit programme came to be. In the 1960s, Korolev unveiled a grand rocket programme called Soyuz, which was to transform the USSR, as it seemed at the time, into the undisputed leader in the space race.

A week after Gagarin's flight, Wernher von Braun received a letter from President Kennedy, readdressed to him by Vice President Johnson. In this letter, Kennedy asked what the United States had to do to catch up with the Soviets in space, and whether a lunar landing was possible. The German designer, although viewing the situation with some pessimism (the Soviet rocket programme was far ahead of the American equivalent and the technological gulf had reached threatening proportions), proposed to Kennedy a

[17] Gagarin's words are famous for the incorrect choice of verb of motion. The Russian *poekhali* means 'let's go' by land-based transport, as opposed to *poshli* ('let's go' on foot) and *poleteli* ('let's go' by air)

number of radical, but well-argued options. Von Braun, in fact, proposed that the American space programme be switched to a state of emergency, that all forces and all resources be concentrated on one objective and to dramatically expand investment. If that were to happen Braun remarked, America could put a man on the Moon by about 1967–68. Kennedy raised these proposals with Congress on 25 May 1961 and the Apollo programme was born.

However, back in the summer of 1956 Korolev, standing in the thick grass of Baikonur and observing the latest launch, began thinking about the possible creation of a super-heavy rocket to fly to the Moon. When the ambitious lunar plans of the Americans became known, Korolev took up the challenge and, in March 1963, he presented the design for his own spacecraft. There are many who believe that, if it were not for the death of the Chief Designer, who, in addition to his scientific genius, had a wonderful talent for organization and, most importantly, was gifted with a stubbornness bordering on fanatacism, the Soviet Union would have beaten the Americans to the Moon. However, competent experts state that this is not the case. Not one N-1 rocket, designed for a flight to the Moon, had a succesful take-off and the lunar programme was closed down. Instead, the USSR concentrated its efforts on the development of orbital stations. Two rockets, ready for launch at Baikonur, were destroyed but the project director Kuznetsov, despite the absurd orders from above, managed to preserve and mothball 150 engines for different rocket stages. In the 1990s, the Americans bought them for their Atlas rockets.

After the lunar programme was closed down the Baikonur Cosmodrome was to see many different programmes and projects, some implemented but others unrealizable; some with promise and others going nowhere. As a rule they were all initiated by the needs of the defence industry. However, the most successful continued to work on peaceful space exploration. The two most successful programmes are associated with the dramatic, albeit brilliant decline of the Soviet space age. These were the Buran and the Mir programmes. The Soviet Union had been dead for ten years, but an object continued to orbit the Earth, bearing the symbols of a non-existent state. This was the Mir Orbital Space Station, launched in February 1986. The programme of third-generation Mir stations proved that the Soviet Union was the undisputed leader in the creation of orbiting spacecraft and the significance of this was far greater than that of the flights to the Moon.

At present all technological solutions and ready modules for the next, as yet incomplete Mir are being applied in the Russian sector of the International Space Station. Unfortunately, modern Russia is financially not in the position of the USSR to implement space projects of this order of magnitude single-handedly.

Lost in the steppes: this was an apt name for Baikonur in the early 1990s. The cosmodrome was the brainchild of the Soviet strategic military programme and the fall of the superpower had the most catastrophic effect on it. Worst of all, the world's largest cosmodrome found itself belonging to no one, both in a legal and a financial sense. Its status was undetermined, financing from the Russians only came for the organization of space flights, and the Kazakhstan side was not in a position to support the social infrastructure. The entire course of the first half of the 1990s saw a headlong degradation of Leninsk-Baikonur. During this time of uncertainty, Moscow tried to squeeze all it could from commercial flights, without investing in the maintenance of the cosmodrome, while Alma-Ata tried to achieve recognition of its sovereignty over the site.

As a result, in 1994, the two sides reached a compromise: Russia acknowledged Baikonur as the property and sovereign territory of Kazakhstan and entered a twenty-year lease of the cosmodrome.[18] As of 1 January 1995, all mutual debts, including those on the cosmodrome, had been offset and the relationships came to be built on a regular market-based contractual agreement. Russia began to pay rent (including some in the form of weapons, equipment, etc.) and each of the parties contributed about 50 million dollars towards the upkeep of the site's infrastructure. An inventory was taken of the site assets and social protection measures were introduced for the population. In this way, the impression was created

[18] The lease involved an annual payment of 115 million dollars and in 1995 the lease agreement was secured by an inter-governmental 'Agreement on the Status of the City of Baikonur'. However, in fact, the agreement simply reinforced the status quo. Russia paid no money, offsetting the lease payments against the so-called national debt of the Republic of Kazakhstan. In turn, Kazakhstan reckoned on receiving its share from the commercial launches through 'its own cosmodrome'. These rather indeterminate relationships became even more complicated when, at the end of the 1990s there were more frequent instances of falling Proton rockets. Kazakhstan's leaders found themselves under pressure from an outraged ecology-minded public and they used this to push Moscow.

that, from 1999, the cosmodrome would start to function in a proper manner. However, the misadventures of the great cosmodrome were not to end. Russia's financial shortcomings became the talk of the town: Russia had enough money for the oligarchs, but not enough to maintain the cosmodrome, which still enabled the country to be seen as a major world power.

In recent years, Baikonur has been regaining its previous status, albeit not very smoothly. Of course, the former gloss cannot be returned to the city, nor enthusiasm to the population, just as the Soviet space power cannot be recovered either. Moreover, events unfolded in such a way that the critical question could arise: will there be a cosmodrome in the next decade? In 2004, Russia and Kazakhstan agreed to extend the lease until the middle of this century, providing the current price of the lease is retained. Nevertheless, despite the insistence of the Russian side to extend the lease, there are serious concerns that, in the mid-term, Russia will turn away from Baikonur as its principal cosmodrome. As we know, Moscow is taking steps to develop cosmodromes in two other locations: Plesetsk and Kapustin Yar.

This is where the geopolitical factor comes into play. All the manoeuvres of the Russian Federation's space defence forces demonstrate that Baikonur retains its strategic military significance for Russia on the same if not on a greater level than in Soviet times. An increasing number of successful launches of intercontinental ballistic missiles (ICBM) have been made from this site and they have shown that the Russian strategic forces are, as before, capable of striking any target on the planet.

Kazakhstan has its own self-interests to be addressed, linked with the fate of Baikonur. Of course, it is inconceivable that the world's largest cosmodrome would be allowed to just disappear. In addition to the clear financial benefits, Baikonur also presents Kazakhstan with a strategic and scientific significance. There was another agreement that was reached between Russia and Kazakhstan – on the creation of the Baiterek space and rocket complex at the cosmodrome, at the site of the Energiya rocket start complex that is currently disused. Baiterek is designed with a high level of ecological safety and is to be used for the Russian Angara rocket. Kazakhstan intends to use this complex to implement its own space programme, with the launch of a national telecommunications satellite. The project cost about 200 million dollars and was completed in 2007.

In this way, Kazakhstan has already become by right a country with a stake in space. The official status of proprietor of the cosmodrome, which belongs to Kazakhstan, had to be and could be filled with real content. Despite its initially modest potential at first glance, Kazakhstan is more than capable of developing several space programmes, train specialists at international centres and finance many projects in conjunction with Russia, the USA, the EU, India and China, and position itself as a country with ambitions in the field of space. In future, this will bring immeasurable political and economic benefits, as the most advanced technologies are concentrated in this sphere. In this way, the preservation of Baikonur is a task of both political and strategic importance. We should also remember that this is a critical military and space site, which ensures the security of both Russia and Kazakhstan.

IT'S NOT YET ISLAM

In connection with the tragic events of 2001 and the years that followed, which in world public opinion are often associated with the not unknown theory of the 'clash of civilizations', a few words should be devoted to Islam in Kazakhstan (and in Central Asia as a whole), as countries with such names (ending in -stan) are usually associated with Islam (or worse still, with Islamism). In so doing it is somehow forgotten that Kazakhstan was, until relatively recently, a Soviet republic, where religion (Islam included), if not banned, was restricted in every way possible by the authorities. But let us take things one at a time.

As noted earlier, Islam came to Kazakhstan in the eighth century together with the Arabian cavalry. In 751, at a battle on the River Talas in southern Kazakhstan, the Arabs and their Turkic tribe allies stopped the Chinese from attacking deep into Central Asia. Strictly speaking, it was this date that is considered to be the starting point for the history of Islam in the region, although certain researchers believe the seventh century to be the earliest date that Islam was present in Central Asia. However, the region was actually really Islamized later, during the eleventh and twelfth centuries, where many pre-Islamic cultural and religious traditions of the Turkic peoples were preserved. The history of Central Asian Islam is distinguished by two principal trends: Sufism and Jadidism. Sufism played the alternative role of a social organization and a form of local resistance to alien hegemony. It was Sufism that played a major role in the spread of Islam; through Sufi missionaries, Islam was introduced among the Kazakhs and the Kyrgyz in the fifteenth century. In the future, Sufism played an important role in organizing the spiritual and political resistance to Russian rule, both in tsarist and Soviet times. The oldest orders in the region were Yassawi (founded in the mid-twelfth century by Ahmed Yasavi, traditionally deemed to be the first Turkic mystic) and Nakshbandiya (founded in the fourteenth century).

As regards the phenomenon of Sufism, it is believed to have evolved in the non-Arabic space of the Islamic world. The contradictions between Sufism and official Islam intensified in the ninth century. The Sufi strove wherever they could to establish their monastic structures, which in time began to render a considerable political, economic and financial influence on the world around them. The Sufi made the inclusion of a messianic figure (*Mahdi*) into their teachings the key principle of Shi'ism. The active propaganda of the Sufi sheikhs, who moved from town to town and from country to country, incorporated various elements from other religions and tried to form their own interpretation of the Hadith, which led to unavoidable confrontation with official Islam. In the tenth century, the relationship between Sufism and Orthodox Sunnism came to a head. In the twelfth century, Sufism incorporated all the various associations into a well-organized system, which led in the following century to its transformation into a mass, international movement. The most widespread form of the organization of the Sufi were the orders (*tarika*), while the form of spiritual influence was the religious messages (*baraka*).

The internal hierarchy of Sufism was based on subordination to the advisers and mentors: the sheikhs (Pirs and Marabouts) of the scholars (Murids, Dervish and Fakirs). The Sufi community was known as the *Ikhvan* and it consisted of an internal, closer circle of associates. The major Sufi orders were the Kadiriya and the Yasavia. The latter experienced a considerable influence from other Asian religions and even from Shamanism; in essence it was a Turkic order.

Another major Central-Asian order was the Nakshbandiya, founded in Bukhara in the fourteenth century. This was considered to be the youngest and the most loyal order to Orthodox Islam. It became the most widespread order in central and southern Asia and, more recently, in the West. Contacts with Hinduism and other elements of Pantheism had a significant influence upon the Sufi ideology, as we know. With time, following conquest and resettlement, the Sufi orders came to Europe. Thus, Nakshbandiya became very popular among the European intellectuals who adopted Islam. Some of them became missionaries themselves, and active preachers of Sufism.

By the time the Kazakh Khanate was formed and during its blossoming from the fifteenth to the seventeenth centuries, the Kazakh elite and aristocracy had already become Islamized. However, on the whole the population was wholly indifferent to the norms of official Islam and they saw themselves as Muslims on a purely nominal level. Spiritual life was dominated by various forms of Shamanism, the cult of the sky, the spirits of ancestors and holy places (*Khazret*). Therefore, Sufism, with its mystic and hidden paganism, found a living echo in the Kazakh nomads. Needless to say, there was a complete lack of any form of restriction and segregation of women, widespread in other parts of the Muslim world, including some of the Kazakhs' immediate neighbours. The praying five times a day (*namaz*) was seen in the Kazakh steppe as an onerous and unnecessary formality. In this way, the Kazakhs deservedly acquired the title of 'bad Muslims' from other peoples, a term they use with pride to this day.

With time the pressure, of Islamization, coming from the south, subsided and the Kazakhs found themselves left to their own devices. However, the threat of Islamization suddenly reappeared among the Kazakhs, from where it was to be least expected. At the end of the eighteenth century, when about half the area of Kazakhstan was already annexed by Russia, the Russian Empress Catherine II conceived the idea of 'civilizing' the wild nomads, encouraging them to embrace Islam rather then Christianity, as one would have assumed. However, on this occasion the role of religious missionaries was played by Tatar mullahs, representatives of a people whose language was very close to that of the Kazakhs. The Tatars by that time already had two hundred and fifty years of exchanging places with the Russians, transforming themselves from the upper classes into the vassals of the Russian crown and they were faithful champions of the Russian policy offensive being applied in Siberia and Central Asia. They also adopted the role of the bearers of Islam in the Kazakh steppe, but, as it happened, they were more successful in popularizing their cuisine and their women, thus considerably enriching the gene pool of the Kazakh nation in the process.

After Russia finally conquered Central Asia, the European influence was greatly intensified in the region, which in turn called into being a reformatory movement in Islam, which acquired the name Jadidism. The impulses of the Jadidistic movement came from the Caucasus and the Crimea.

The new movement had two aspects to it and it followed two objectives: on the one hand, it aimed to raise the education of the Muslim population of the Russian Empire to a modern level and bring it to unified standards; on the other hand it aimed to unite the Turkic people 'from the Bosphorous to the Kashgar', on a common cultural and linguistic basis, partly by way of the introduction of a common Turkic alphabet. In future, the battle between Jadidism and the advocates of the old method (the Kadims) grew into a political flat plane. The Bolsheviks found many supporters among the Jadidistic intelligentsia, while the Basmachi[19] had a slogan during the civil war: death to the wrongdoers and the Jadids! However, it was later revealed that the Jadids supported nationalistic rather than class-based ideals, which led to their departure from Muslim communism.

It should be said that the majority of the Kazakhs supported the communist ideas. They willingly fought with the Red Army, sorting out relationships with the Basmachi, who were formed predominantly from their neighbours the Uzbeks and Tajiks. However, there were also Kazakh clans who did not support the Revolution and who left for Chinese Turkestan, Afghanistan and Iran.

In the 1920s, a campaign was inspired in Central Asia to secularize education, free women and attack Islam (*Khudjum*). In 1937–39, almost all Jadidistic intellectuals were eliminated and the Sufi orders became the centre for resistance to Soviet atheism. Soviet power destroyed the Sufi shrines in the Fergana Valley and drove the traditional Sufi doctrine for the region underground, although it was in the Soviet period that the Kadiriya order gained a foothold in Central Asia, which had appeared in the region together with Igushi and Chechens, deported from the Caucasus.

Leading roles in the Central-Asian Sufi orders were often occupied by women. The Kadiriya was especially widespread across

[19] The Basmachi were partisan insurgents in Soviet Central Asia during the civil war of 1918–24. The Basmachi called themselves mujaheddins (fighters of the faith), just like the Mujahads in Afghanistan. The result of all these battles for the faith is well known – 11 September 2001.

Kazakhstan after 1945 and it subsequently continued to increase its influence. During the Second World War, Islam, just as the Orthodox Church, saw a certain relaxing of restrictions, although under Krushchev the attacks on religion were resurrected with renewed vigour. Under Brezhnev, the reinforcement of national cultures and the growth of nationalism had a side-effect in the intensification of the growth of interest in the Islamic legacy of the Central-Asian peoples. At this time the church and the mosque were under the full control of the state and other Soviet institutions, such as the party and the KGB. A popular joke of that time told of the priest who was forced to return his communist party membership card as a punishment for poor propaganda work on his part. However, the actual truth of the matter, and your author has been the witness to this, was that church ministers who wished to obtain academic and theological degrees, were forced, on the same basis as everyone else, to sit master's examinations, which included such an indispensible attribute as the study of Marxist (i.e. atheist) disciplines.

The Gorbachev era witnessed a strengthening of the positions of so-called official Islam and its final structuring under several spiritual forms of governance. In parallel, there was a demarcation of the official and unofficial Islam of the Sufi. The most dramatic indications of an Islamic renaissance in Central Asia after the fall of the USSR involve the increase in the number of mosques (by the end of the century the number had increased from 37 to 100 in Kazakhstan and from 260 to 5,000 in the region as a whole) and the restoration of the Hajj. However, the contact of local Islam with that on the outside had a dangerous effect: the advent of the Wahhabi in Central Asia. As official Islam in the Central-Asian republics began to appeal to the Sufi legacy as a part of the cultural and national legacy (especially in Kazakhstan), there was an intensification of opposition between Sufism and Wahhabism, where the latter has been openly persecuted in Uzbekistan since 1997.

The USA closely tracked the possible intensification of Islam in Central Asia in the early 1990s. The conclusions made by USA were unexpected and sounded reassuring for the West: despite the fact that 50% of Uzbeks and Kazakhs and 45% of Kyrgyzis see themselves as true Muslims, only one in five Uzbeks or Kyrgyzis practise their religion and with Kazakhs this number is lower still.

Nevertheless, Islam has become one of the most important elements in the formation of a new national identity for the people of Central Asia. And yet this process has a very contradictory nature: Islamic organizations are under strict state control, religious parties are banned and government institutions are distinctly secular in their nature. In order to create a certain spiritual counterweight in their countries, from time to time the leaders of new states render demonstrative support for the Orthodox Church. The constitutions of the republics of Central Asia secure a secular nature for the government. The Islamic factor for the new, independent, states of the region also possesses a foreign policy dimension. While all the republics have joined the Organization of the Islamic Conference and established relations with the Arab world and other Islamic countries, relations with Russia, China, the USA and Europe play an important role for them.

In making a general assessment of the evolution of Islam in Central Asia, the conclusion can be made that, over many centuries, this region has been the centre of Islamic philosophy, science and theology. In the Soviet period, religion was almost entirely subordinate to and placed under the control of the state. Its elements were only preserved on an individual or local level, in certain customs and domestic ceremonies. Islam today is now officially proclaimed as a part of the cultural and historical heritage in all the states of the region, although the government is trying to keep Islam under its control in the style of the Soviet era. Any attempts to politicize Islam or to turn it into a force in opposition to authority are suppressed immediately.

As far as the Kazakhs are concerned, they have not betrayed their national character: Islam continues to be a cultural and historical abstraction, an empty formality that should be observed, so as not to offend one's elders. In real life religion plays no part at all, although there are now more outward signs of the presence of a Muslim culture than there were some twenty years ago.

Open displays of piety are considered bad form, especially in the presence of representatives of other faiths or from another ethnic origin. In 2001, Kazakhstan was unexpectedly visited by Pope John-Paul II, which generated a sharp rise in the interest in religion. As a result, Kazakhstan has declared itself a world centre of religious tolerance and holds conferences in its new capital city for representatives of all the world's faiths.

Such a demonstration of religious tolerance is only possible, it has to be said, in a country that is completely devoid of any religiousness. Therefore, we will leave it up to you to answer the question:

are Kazakhs Muslims in the generally-accepted sense, and is Kazakhstan an Islamic country? However, the answer is clear for all to see.

HOW TO DO BUSINESS IN KAZAKHSTAN

This section is not only about, and not as much about, Kazakhstan's economy as may at first appear. For several years now, starting from the turn of the new century, Kazakhstan has been attracting international attention with its economic successes, both alleged and actual. Local reformers attribute these successes to themselves, Western experts and advisers from the IMF, the World Bank and the German IFO Institute believe that they promoted the generation of the correct strategy on the part of the Kazakh Government. Neo-liberals gloat over the miraculous force of market reforms on the Kazakhstan example, while left-wing economists praise Kazakhstan's leaders for the intervention of the state. Kazakhstan's neighbours are indignant and green with envy, while Russian economists hold up Kazakhstan and its financial system as an example to their government.

All of them are right in their own way. Kazakhstan has indeed conducted market reforms, at times painful, and it has considerably liberalized its economy. Then, however, there was a partial return to a policy of state intervention in economic or, more specifically, socio-economic processes. Altogether this had a complicated but on the whole positive effect. Real successes combined with an intelligent image campaign and economic failures in other post-Soviet states (plus the excellent raw materials and oil resources) have promoted the advent of the legend of the 'Kazakh economic miracle'.

There is a long history behind this subject. Back in 1915, German economist Reinhardt Junge wrote a book on the Westernization of Russian Turkestan. In future his recipes were used literally by the Bolsheviks, conducting the modernization of the region in their uncompromising way. Back at the start of the twentieth century Europe's attention was directed to Kazakhstan's rich resources and potential, although at first the immense desert-like Kazakh steppes could not instil such optimism. However, in just fifty years, in the 1960s, Western Sovietologists admired the speed of the economic transformation of Kazakhstan. The French economists Louis Blanchard and Henri Chambre from the National Institute of Statistics and Economics declared Kazakhstan to be one of the most important cornerstones of the growth of the Soviet Union and its raw materials and industrial base, with an opportunity to transform into a developed industrial region. This opinion was shared by Violet Connolly from Oxford with her book *Beyond the Urals*, in which she wrote about the turning of the Asiatic part of the USSR into a new region of economic growth on the planet. Naturally, Kazakhstan's speedy advance in an economic sense could not but attract the attention of this major specialist, whose opinion was valued, among others, by the British Foreign Office.

Naturally, all of these successes were reported in the context of a growing threat of the 'aggressive Soviet power', which was what kept the Sovietologists at their most busy. Ten years later and they were to begin writing about the rise of nationalism and the resurrection of Islam, foretelling the inevitable fall of the Soviet Union (yet no one apart from the far-sighted Helene Carrère d'Encausse could imagine that this could occur so quickly). It is worthy of note that in any event attention was directed to the unprecedented economic development of Kazakhstan.

As already mentioned, Kazakhstan performed several roles at once, all created for it by the Soviet regime. The republic was the agricultural, primarily grain and meat, storehouse for the Soviet Union, a raw material base for an enormous industrial complex, encompassing the Urals and Siberia. With its raw materials, Kazakhstan supported the empire's uranium industry and played an important role in configuring the chemical industry. In so doing Kazakhstan became one of the most important parts of the Soviet strategic military programmes: nuclear, missile, chemical and biological. From the point of view of propaganda, Kazakhstan fulfilled the role of an 'incubator for internationalism' and a model for conducting a 'wise' national policy of the communist party. Finally, now in the time of Gorbachev's rule, Kazakhstan came to be spoken of as the Soviet Kuwait of the future, with knowledge spreading of the huge hydrocarbon reserves in the western part of the republic and on the petroleum shelf of the Caspian Sea.

The tempestuous events of the early 1990s, with the instant and universal collapse of the Soviet economy, could not but have an effect on Kazakhstan. However, the impact was mitigated by Kazakhstan's raw material resources, metals in particular, which helped it withstand the impact and get through the seemingly catastrophic fall of the previous system. Banking on the fact that the raw materials sectors would help to accumulate the strength to get through the difficult but necessary reforms fully paid off in strategic prospects for the future.[20]

For the entire duration of the first half of the 1990s a big game was being played out around Kazakhstani oil. The geopolitical positions of many powers were involved in the matter, along with the interests of major transnational companies, and grand geoeconomic transport and communications projects appeared on the scene. The result was the arrival of transnational companies (TNC), the operations of which appeared to cast a dark cloud over the image of Western capitalism in the eyes of the population, over the reputation of certain high-ranking politicians in Kazakhstan and which had a significant influence on the relations of Kazakhstan with the great powers of the USA, Russia, the European Union and, a little later, China. In a strange twist of fate, it was not income from oil sales that promoted the recovery of Kazakhstan's economy.

The economic strategy banked on the macro-stabilization of the national economy, the development of the financial sector and the banking system, the release of entrepreneurial energy through market reforms and the raising of finance. The most complex task on this path was, of course, the introduction of a national currency and all that followed the adoption of this financial responsibility. Complications lay in wait for the young Kazakhstani currency, not only in the domestic economy but also, to no lesser degree, in the international arena. Kazakhstan, broadly dependent upon imports and many export items, was totally unable to isolate its own current situation from external influence.

To some extent, it was fortunate that Kazakhstan's independent currency and financial system was constructed in the early 1990s, when the whole world had witnessed the calamitous and bitter consequences for many countries in Latin America and Africa which resulted from following the recommendations and strict requirements of the IMF in the 1970s and 1980s. To ensure the same did not happen in Kazakhstan, the republic's leaders decided to invite a group of independent experts to provide the Government

---

[20] However, no account is made for the many victims of these reforms, linked by their reliance on the state budget. These are the pensioners, the military, doctors and teachers. And this is despite the fact that the market principles did work in the spheres of their professional activity. Furthermore, a monstrous thing happened from the point of view of traditional Soviet morality: the division of society into the rich and the poor.

with a more or less objective and, most importantly, independent analysis of IMF recommendations and predict how expedient or not it would be to follow the Fund's directions. As the IMF is sometimes perceived to be under US control, it was a natural thing to invite Europeans as advisers, presenting an alternative financial and economic force in the world to the Americans.

Young Kazakhstani financiers, who still had close connections with German specialists from the time of their studies in West Germany, proposed candidates from the German Institute For Economic Research in Munich. Over seven years these experts were faced with the task of observing first hand the formation of Kazakhstan's currency and financial system, and to protect them from the destructive influence of the IMF's counsel. What happened at that time was beneficial only to domestic and international profiteers, yet the IMF insisted on continuing its previous liberal policy. However, the German experts stubbornly insisted on the combination of proportions in conducting a macro- and micro-economic policy. German advisers made a precise diagnosis of the catastrophic position of the Kazakhstani economy and revealed the reasons behind it: the effect of a so-called double shock therapy, where the macro-economic shock overlays the shock of the period of transformation.

The Germans believe that the young Kazakhstani financiers fell into a high-interest-rate trap, meaning they set a goal of raising capital from the population as a form of domestic investment. However, the population's lack of trust in the banking system at that time was considerable. They called this contradiction a dead-end street between the macro- and micro-economic policy. In this way, at different stages of the development of Kazakhstan's financial system, the German advisers, in turn, pointed to the weak points in the economic policy and to the traps that were lying in wait for them along the way. And almost every time the advice of the independent experts contradicted the recommendations of the IMF. In the early 1990s, it was a problem of stabilizing price-growth dynamics; in the middle of the decade, it was a matter of budget policy; in the latter half of the 1990s, it was the use of revenue from raw material resources. By the end of the century Kazakhstan was faced with a new task: pushing through pension reforms.

Thanks, to a great extent, to the experience of the German specialists and their advice, Kazakhstan's financial system, now considered to be the best in the CIS, acquired the features that ensured it would be effective: an assurance of payment discipline, support of transparency of financial operations and so on. Even to the untrained eye, Kazakhstan's financial policy demonstrates a strong political will, a clear understanding of its strategic objectives, its overall mission and potential threats. This factor would have been impossible if it were not for the close cooperation between the Kazakhstani financiers and the German experts.

The last time the viewpoints of the IMF and the German specialists collided was on the eve of the Asian crisis. The German consultants raised the alarm as early as March 1998, insisting that protective measures be taken to prevent the consequences of the devaluation of the Asian currencies. The Germans saw no other way out than to devalue the tenge.[21] The IMF, to which the Kazakhstani Government was more inclined to listen at that time, insisted on supporting high interest rates and aggressive operations on the open markets.

Thus, in the period when our national currency was being formed it had godparents and nannies, standing on either side of the little tenge's cradle. These nannies were the representatives of the IMF and the German Institute of Economic Research, represented by their independent experts. Here, the latter tried to protect the tenge from the overly strict and radical advice and recommendations of the IMF. Put in simple terms, the Fund demanded that the baby should bathe in ice-cold water from its first days, while the Germans suggested adding some warm water to the bath.

In 1997, there was a fundamental clash on pension reform between the independent advisers and the World Bank. The German experts accused the World Bank and other international institutions of actively supporting a transfer to a new funded pension scheme, without warning the Kazakhstani Government that such a move could intensify political problems in the country. For the Government of the republic, which heeded advice from outside without due consideration, the most important objective then was to liquidate the accumulated debt and resolve the issue of non-payment.

---

[21] The tenge is the national currency of the Republic of Kazakhstan, introduced in November 1993.

At this time, the need arose to develop the processing sectors in Kazakhstan, to avoid dependence on raw material exports. Leaving the country at the start of the new century, the German advisers gave the Kazakhstani leadership two pieces of advice. The first involved getting rid of the tutelage of the IMF and financial and loan dependence on the Fund as soon as possible. Kazakhstan followed this advice and fulfilled all its obligations to the IMF ahead of schedule. The second piece of advice involved getting Kazakhstan and its economy away from dependence on raw materials. All the governments of Kazakhstan, wherever possible, have tried to heed this advice and recommendations and, sometimes, even ultimatums from one side or another, and to take them into account. However, in reality it seems that at the heart of our financial strategy there were strict imperatives, dictated by life and the pressing tasks of the present.

The principal result of this early history of the tenge's formation is that it has been possible to create an efficient and operational banking and financial system and generate skills in control and management over the macro- and micro-economic situation. As such, Kazakhstan was already prepared for new storms on the world's markets. The main danger came from the dependence on raw material exports and, through this, from the unpredictable and uncontrolled structure of the global markets.

The process of economic transformation in Kazakhstan is a graphic example of the difficulties that have to be overcome on the way to a market economy, even for new independent states with the richest of resources. The country's leaders inherited a situation that gave real grounds for optimism. The economy was diversified in nature and a reasonably well-developed processing industry and agricultural sector presented potential for a smooth transition to independence, by satisfying the material requests of the population to an extent that would preserve political stability.

Kazakhstan's decision to develop its oil resources by creating international consortia attracted the majority of the world's major oil companies. This strategy led to the arrival of many international players, who strove to assert an influence both on the country's government and on its companies. Many of them sought a way to become friends with the regime. There were many obstacles along the road to foreign investment, which Kazakhstan did not create itself. Thus, for a long time, Kazakhstani politicians were unable to independently move forward to deal with the challenge of transporting energy resources.

On the way to achieving its successes, the country's leadership had to resolve four tasks: gain economic independence from Russia and other post-Soviet states, privatize available resources and companies without damaging the country's ability to sustain itself and fulfil social obligations, stimulate foreign investment and, finally, ensure that government officials demonstrate political will and discipline themselves and their relatives to stop corruption becoming an insurmountable hurdle for the functioning of the economy.

The country's economic strategy focused on the spheres of the economy for which foreign investment had priority: energy, especially oil and gas; food industry; gold mining; oil refining; and non-ferrous metal mining and processing. The central focus of attention was the United States and Europe, where Kazakhstan presented itself as a Europeanized society, ensuring unhindered access to the markets of Central Asia and regions beyond. In endeavouring to appear in an attractive light to Korean, Japanese and other Asian investors, Kazakhstan stressed its 'Asianness', just as it strove to combine capitalism and authoritarianism, following the example of certain 'Asian Tigers'. Kazakhstan courted Turkey and, to a lesser extent, the oil-producing countries of the Middle East, reminding them of their common ethnic (with Turkey) and religious (with other Muslim countries) identity, without rousing the spectres of pan-Turkism or pan-Islamism.

Nevertheless, the Government in Astana does have grounds for optimism. Under a certain opacity in the business atmosphere in Kazakhstan, considerable volumes of foreign investment continue to pour into the country, compared with other newly-independent states. The economy is witnessing some improvement, inflation is generally under control and from the end of the 1990s, production has been on the rise. Moreover, unlike the majority of its neighbours, Kazakhstan has managed to preserve mutual understanding with the World Bank and other international financial institutions on most issues.

Economic growth in Kazakhstan had more than simply economic consequences. It also touched on the development of domestic politics. The decision to move to a market economy had political consequences which, in turn, led to the advent of new players. The next generation of the political elite is now growing up from within the heart of the economy and this trend is already beginning to show. Ministerial appointments today are made taking into account the Government's need for key economic groups, predominantly linked with powerful lobbying from these economic structures. The same trend is also traced on a regional level, where major companies often prove capable of putting forward their own people for inclusion in local administrations, to protect their own interests in the first instance.

On the whole, the actions of foreign companies in the Kazakhstani part of the Caspian are promoted both by predicted and proven resources of this region, and by the attractive conditions, offered by the Government under an improvement of the favourable investment climate in the country. About 60% of foreign investment falls to enterprises in the oil-and-gas complex. The policy of raising foreign investment into Kazakhstan's economy and the oil-and-gas complex is distinguished primarily by a striving to lessen its dependence on Russia as much as possible. The specific nature of Kazakhstan's relations with Russia involve the fact that both countries are natural competitors on the world markets for raw materials.

A characteristic feature of investment projects in the republic's fuel and energy complex is the scale and the rates at which industry is being privatized. In almost two years about 90% of the country's industry was sold. This is where Kazakhstan's policy of raising investment differs from that of other post-Soviet countries, which rely on new investment projects, while preserving majority state ownership in the fuel-and-energy sector.

Finally, there is one more feature of the investment policy that is specific to Kazakhstan amd that is the diversity of foreign investors. Together with this, as the number of foreign companies operating in the region increases, the probability of their interests conflicting also rises, both with domestic companies and amongst themselves. The most promising raw hydrocarbon deposits have been given to foreign companies to develop. The deposits and fields that belong to Kazakhstan are in an initial production phase and considerable capital investment would be required to support decent yield volumes.

The advent of an economic growth point in the Caspian, speaking in the language of twentieth-century economists, in the form of the Caspian oil boom, will most likely have as its main socio-economic consequence a push towards development in other spheres of the economy of Kazakhstan and of Central Asia as a whole. The matter concerns the accompanying sectors, service sphere, the production of goods and the necessary equipment, the development of the transport infrastructure, and so on.

So what role in this mini-revolution will be allocated to Kazakhstan? It will be faced with taking on the regulation and direction of the principal vectors of economic growth in the region and deciding in practice in which form and at what rate the region's economy will be developing on mutually beneficial terms. This mission can be compared with a locomotive, tasked with 'pulling' its carriages up steep hills. Naturally, this locomotive must have economic weight and financial power and Kazakhstan should gain these properties from the Caspian dividends and, most importantly, from broad integration into the system of international economic links, which will inevitably follow the full-scale use of the resources of the Caspian Sea and entry to the World Trade Organization (WTO).

As far as Kazakhstan's involvement in globalization is concerned, it is very similar to the position of other countries in the post-Soviet space, although there are essential distinguishing features. It is assumed that they are presented with three possible scenarios for entering the process of globalization. The first involves the country's partial inclusion into the system of international economic ties with a turning away from the values - political and cultural - as components of the process. This is a contradictory variation and one which is hard to fulfil on the basis of the mutual dependence of all factors of globalization: economic, political and cultural.

The second variation assumes a forced entry into globalization, meaning the rapid adoption of its values and practices. Such a scenario is hard to imagine and, what is more, it would trigger the rejection of its cultural identity and political independence. Finally, there is the third variation, which comes down to a departure from globalization, the continuation of development under the Soviet model, which is based on the supply of raw materials in exchange for technologies and consumer goods. Such isolation or semi-isolation would lead to a finale that we already know: the stagnation of the economy with the corresponding social and political consequences. It seems that we have to seek a new model for Kazakhstan in the context of the current environment of globalization, which takes all three variations into account, the elements of which are already in play.

In this way, despite all the successes (at times relative) in its economic development, Kazakhstan is still having to face up to many problems. However, at the same time, such problems often bring about potential options for foreign investors, that is if you reckon on joining their number. If the strategic spheres of the economy of Kazakhstan are already in place, and we class large-scale industry, oil-and-gas, metallurgy, ore and a number of others, mostly primary-product sectors in their number, in prospect there are surely an enormous number of niches still unoccupied. Agriculture in Kazakhstan is at a critical stage in its development. Wine-making, once a flourishing industry in the south of the country and thoughtlessly destroyed in the Gorbachev era, is now crying out to be resurrected. The Soviet potential, which managed to survive the difficult 1990s, has now exhausted itself. New management is required, new technologies, especially selection technologies, and simply new equipment. Potentially, Kazakhstan could turn into a grain and meat provider, not only for its immediate neighbours and within the CIS, but also for the entire European Union.

Sectors such as tourism, infrastructure development, construction, transport, communications and trading are in need of Western-level experienced managers. Furthermore, Kazakhstan has the opportunity to apply and develop latest state-of-the-art technologies, including space, biological, atomic, chemical and nanotechnologies. On the whole, the economic development of Kazakhstan demonstrates a potential, under which, following the strategic sectors should come the fundamental development of the accompanying sectors and service provision. All of this reveals wonderful opportunities for cooperation with international partners, and these could perhaps include you, the reader of this book.

In Place of a Conclusion: Love this Country

And so, our story of Kazakhstan, a country stretching across the expanses of Eurasia, is nearing its end. It would be more correct to say it is only just beginning, at least for you, the reader. As the well-known saying goes, it is better to see something once than to hear about it a hundred times, and we would be delighted to see you in the land of the Kazakhs.

Perhaps something from our tale will strike you as exaggerated, while something else may appear understated. Nevertheless, you will be welcomed in any capacity: a curious tourist, potential partner or interested guest.

As you have read, Kazakhstan and its people have lived through a difficult history, which was often excessively harsh on them. The geography and the climate dictated that at the dawn of history the people who settled on this land were forced to fight for their survival. The fight for survival in adverse natural conditions was then supplemented with a struggle against a multitude of opponents. Kazakhstan has experienced the fall of many eras and civilizations, the most poignant of which was the separation from its old nomadic identity. Nevertheless, many of its symbols still survive to this day. The last trauma was only very recently, in 1991, and it still resonates painfully in the hearts of those who were raised on ideas of equality, justice and brotherhood.

However, history waits for no man and time moves inexorably on. Today, Kazakhstan is trying to resolve several challenges simultaneously: to modernize, technically, ideologically and morally, to build a national government and to integrate into the new world of globalization. These objectives are closely interconnected and, at times, they contradict one another.

A transition zone in a human, cultural and geographical sense, Kazakhstan today is the product of a peculiar synthesis of different ways to manage an economy, subordinating nomadic livestock farming, the agriculture of settled peoples and the industrial development of rich, raw material resources. Finally, it joins various cosmogonical and religious concepts (Shamanism, Islam and Christianity) with certain political and social constructions, including or excluding tradition and modernity. As a result, the internal organization of Kazakhstan is a full reflection of its original state, emerging out of the synthesis of the European model, transplanted from Russia, and its inner Turko-Muslim core, that has been preserved in the traditional sphere. All of this has created a polyethnic and multi-faith Kazakhstani society.

Kazakhstan today is considered to be the most successful economy among the countries of the CIS. The process of economic transformation in Kazakhstan is a graphic example of the difficulties that have to be overcome on the way to a market economy, even for newly-independent states with the richest of resources. The country's leaders inherited a situation that gave real grounds for optimism. The economy was diversfied in nature and a reasonably well-developed processing industry and agricultural sector presented potential for a smooth transition to independence, by satisfying the material requests of the population to an extent that would preserve political stability.

However, the republic's economy has come a long way and this path is characterized by a dramatic fall in production and a high level of inflation at the beginning of the 1990s. But by the end of the 1990s, Kazakhstan had come through a phase of macroeconomic stabilization, the creation of a financial system and the privatization of major sectors of the economy. From then until the present, the economy of Kazakhstan has been in the ascendancy.

Economic reforms, implemented under the leadership of President Nursultan Nazarbaev, have led to serious sociopolitical changes. Kazakhstani business now has young entrepreneurs, who have graduated from famous institutes in Moscow or who hold degrees in economics, finance and the engineering sciences from the English-speaking world. In the early 1990s, many of them became the owners of small and medium-sized businesses or banks. They acquired the mentality of a liberal market economy and they were ready and able to run their business without state subsidies. These representatives of the younger generation received the best education, they established international contacts and they were not burdened with the ideological ballast of the Soviet period.

In Kazakhstan, just as in other liberal countries, there is a political opposition and no one denies this fact. To a great extent the advent of an opposition was the result of the economic reforms, and here we should also mention the political pragmatism of the political elite in Kazakhstan, which coopts its rivals, not in the interests of preserving a monopoly of power, but in order to bind the principal political forces so as to avoid internal conflicts. In its turn, the opposition adheres to principles of loyalty and corporativity, if it wishes to take part in the political process. The Government has picked up and partly even implemented one of the central demands of the opposition, namely reform of electoral law but, at the same time, it has ensured the inclusion of mechanisms that stabilize the process of a change of power.

Kazakhstan has other problems, too. On a regional level in Kazakhstan there is a significant disproportion in population numbers, structure and development. On the one hand there are regions with a predominantly rural population and with a principally agricultural and old industrial structure. On the other hand, there are regions with large urban populations, which also have significant mineral deposits as well as competitive industries.

The move of the capital in 1997, from Alma-Ata to Astana, located in the centre of the country, increased the reach of central government and facilitated its task of day-to-day control over the low-populated northern and western regions.

So what is today's Kazakhstan? It is a country that has successfully rid itself of the negative elements of the Soviet legacy; it is a country that is building an open and democratic society with a liberal spirit. Kazakhstan is already coming out of the transition phase, where economic reforms come before those of a political nature. Encountering many problems and difficulties, Kazakhstan and its political elite have learnt to resolve them and this should be recognized as the principal achievement of the post-Soviet era. The next major objective is the consolidation of society.

The situation regarding the language is also a positive contributing factor as regards the unification of the country, not least because of the actual linguistic homogeneity of the Kazakh language and the absence of dialects. Russian as a means of communication for all ethnic groups is also a unifying factor. However, in recent years, Kazakhstan has seen the advent of a third lingua franca: English, the language of international communication, is actively encouraged by the authorities. The language problem is closely linked with the process of acculturalization, which promoted and continues to promote the cultural convergence of the two main ethnic groups, the Kazakhs and the Russians, with the adoption one from the other of various elements of everyday life, behaviour and cultural stereotypes.

The only departure in terms of strengthening the unity of Kazakhstan and preserving its political structure was the decision to combine a unitary government with a powerful presidency. The history of the Kazakh steppe is full of examples, when a threat from outside has rallied the nation and led to national and state unity. A similar situation can be observed today. The political elite rallied through common interests to preserve the state sovereignty and territorial integrity of the country. Kazakhstan's politicians operate pragmatically and avoid any ideological confrontration.

In the politics of Kazakhstan, the following priorities are clear: the creation of an effective government, capable of surviving under the globalization of international relations, one that is an economic leader in the region in its role of 'snow leopard'[1] and one that remains true to its Eurasian surroundings.

And what next for Kazakhstan? If we knew the answer to this question, this book would probably not have been written. Despite the positive psychological mind-set of the young Kazakhstani nation and its successes in building a new national identity and a successful economy, there are many things that give cause for concern. Kazakhstan remains as before in the centre of Eurasia, surrounded by a complex mix of neighbours, some of which are true giants.

Despite close links with the West, Kazakhstan has been unable to break the thread that binds it with the East, including the Muslim world. Furthermore, society is still not totally rid of the traces of communism. Those with nostalgic ideas look in hope to the north. At the same time, having lived through a whole series of culture shocks, Kazakhstan today is a successful synthesis of the Asian East and the European West. Kazakhstan has all it needs to become a flourishing democratic state characterized by its ethnic diversity, extensive territory, multi-faceted economy and well-educated population.

---

[1] The snow leopard is an unofficial symbol of Kazakhstan.

And yet Kazakhstan has that something which ensures optimism remains high. There are more and more young people in the country, who look with true faith to the future; they build this future and they represent this future in the present. For these young people, who have grown up and have fully developed in what is already an independent Kazakhstan, our worries and doubts mean far less. They are optimistic and, at the same time, not so naïve as to fail to understand that Kazakhstan's future fully depends on them, on their will, their professionalism and their persistence in achieving their goals.

From the outside world all that they are hoping for is for their country to be understood and loved. So, fall in love with this country!

Appendix: Some Demographic Facts and Figures

Kazakhstan	EU	UK	USA
AREA (km2)			
2,724,900 (9th)	4,324,782	244,820 (79th)	9,826,630 (4th)
POPULATION			
15,217,711 (62nd)	499,673,300	60,975,000 (22nd)	305,776,000 (3rd)

LAND BOUNDARIES
Total: 12,185 km
Border countries: China 1,533km, Kyrgyzstan 1,224 km, Russia 6,846 km, Turkmenistan 379 km, Uzbekistan 2,203km

RELIGIONS
Muslim 47%, Russian Orthodox 44%, Protestant 2%, other 7%

ETHNIC GROUPS
Kazakh 53.4%, Russian 30%, Ukrainian 3.7%, Uzbek 2.5%, German 2.4%, Tatar 1.7%, Uygur 1.4%, other 4.9% (1999 census)

Further Reading

IN ENGLISH

Abazov R., *Culture and Customs of the Central Asian Republics.* Westport (CT), London: Greenwood Press, 2007. xiv+286 pp.
Akiner S., *The Formation of Kazakh Identity from Tribe to Nation-State.* London: Royal Institute of International Affairs, 1995. 83 pp.
Allison R., Jonson L. (eds), *Central Asian Security. The New International Context.* London, Washington: RIIA/Brooking Institution Press, 2001. xv+279 pp.
Allworth E. (ed.), *Central Asia: A Century of Russian Rule.* New York: Columbia University Press, 1967. 550 pp.
Bacon E. E., *Central Asia under Russian Rule. A Study in Cultural Change.* Ithaca, New York: Cornell University Press, 1966. 273 pp.
Benson L. and Svanberg I. (eds), *The Kazaks of China. Essays on the Ethnic Minority.* Uppsala: Uppsala University Press, 1988. 250 pp.
Benson L., Svanberg I., *China's Last Nomads. The History and Culture of China's Kazaks.* New York: M.E. Sharp, 1998. xiii+251 pp.
Bowyer A. C., *Parliament and Political Parties in Kazakhstan.* Washington, DC: Central Asia-Caucasus Institute & Silk Road Studies Program, 2008. 71 pp.
Burghart D.L., Sabonis-Helf Th. (eds) *In the Tracks of Tamerlane. Central Asia's Path to the Twenty-first Century.* Washington, DC: NDU, 2004. xxii+478 pp.
Brzezinski Z., *The Grand Chessboard. American Primacy and Its Geostrategic Imperatives.* New York: Collins, 1997. xiv+223 pp.
Connolly V., *Beyond the Urals. Economic Development in Soviet Asia.* London: Oxford University Press, 1967. 420 pp.
Chufrin G. (ed.), *The Security of the Caspian Sea Region.* Oxford, New York: Oxford University Press, 2001 (SIPRI). xvi+375 pp.
Cummings S. N., *Kazakhstan. Centre-Periphery Relations.* London: The Royal Institute of International Affairs, 2000. viii+55 pp.
Cummings S. N. (ed.), *Power and Change in Central Asia.* London, New York: Routledge, 2002. viii+158 pp.
Cummings S., *Nursultan Nazarbaev and Presidential Power in Kazakhstan.* New York: Columbia University, 1999.
Daly J. C. K., *Kazakhstan's Emerging Middle Class.* Washington, DC: Central Asia-Caucasus Institute & Silk Road Studies Program, 2008. 100 pp.
Davis van Wie E., Azizian R. (eds), *Islam, Oil and Geopolitics: Central Asia after September 11.* Boulder (CO): Rowman and Littlefield Publishers, 2007. vii+308 pp.

Dekmejian R. H., Simonian H., *Troubled Waters. The Geopolitics of the Caspian Region*. London:Tauris, 2003. 281 pp.

Dixon A., *Kazakhstan: Political Reform and Economic Development*. London: The Royal Institute of International Affairs, 1994. x+42 pp.

Environmental Performance Review: Kazakhstan. Geneva: UNECE, 2001–02.

Everett-Heath T. (ed.), *Central Asia. Aspects of Transition*. London, New York: RoutledgeCurzon, 2003. x+290 pp.

Holm-Halsen J., *Territorial and Ethno-Cultural Self-government in Nation-building in Kazakhstan*. Oslo: Norwegian Institute for Urban and Regional Research, 1997. 100 pp.

Garnett S., Rahr A., Watanabe K. *The New Central Asia. A Report to the Trilateral Commission: 54 (October)*. New York, Paris, Tokyo: The Trilateral Commission, 2000. 79 pp.

George A., *Journey into Kazakhstan. The True Face of the Nazarbayev Regime*. New York: University Press of America, 2001.

Gokay B. (ed.)., *The Politics of Caspian Oil*. Houndmills, Basingstoke, Hampshire, New York: Palgrave, 2001. ix+232 pp.

Gray J., *Kazakhstan: a Review of Farm Restructuring*. Washington, DC: World Bank, 2000.

Jones Luong P., *Economic Decentralization in Kazakhstan: Causes and Consequences*. Yale: Yale University, 2003.

Kleveman L., *The New Great Game. Blood and Oil in Central Asia*. London: Atlantic Books, 2003. xx+283 pp.

Laumulin M., *The Security, Foreign Policy and International Relationship of Kazakhstan after Independence: 1991–2001*. Almaty: KazISS and Friedrich Ebert Stiftung, 2002. 212 pp.

Laumulin M., *Central Asia and the West: the Geopolitical Impact on the Regional Security*. Almaty: KazISS, 2004. 219 pp.

Laumulin M., *The Geopolitics of the Twenty-first Century in Central Asia*. Almaty: KazISS, 2007. 281 pp.

Legvold R. (ed.), *Thinking Strategically. The Major Powers, Kazakhstan, and the Central Asian Nexus*. Cambridge (Mass.), London: The MIT Press, 2003. xii+243 pp.

Nazarbaev N., *Without Right and Left*. London: Class Publishing, 1992.

Martin V., *Law and Custom in the Steppe: The Kazakhs of the Middle Horde and Russian Colonialism in the Nineteenth Century*. London: RoutledgeCurzon, 2001.

Olcott M. B., *The Kazakhs*. 2nd ed. Stanford: Hoover Institution Press, 1995. 388 pp.

Olcott M. B., *Kazakhstan: Unfulfilled Promise*. Washington: Carnegie Endowment, 2002. xii+321 pp.

Olcott M. B., *Central Asia's Second Chance*. Washington, DC: Carnegie Endowment, 2005. xiii+389 pp.

Robbins C., *In Search of Kazakhstan. The Land that Disappeared*. London: Profile Books, 2007. 296 pp.

Rumer B. (ed.), *Central Asia and the New Global Economy*. Armonk, New York, London: M.E. Sharp, 2000. xi+288 pp.

Rumer B. (ed.), *Central Asia: a Gathering Storm?* Armonk, New York, London: M.E. Sharp, 2002. xiii+441 pp.

Rumer B. (ed.), *Central Asia. At the End of Transition*. Armonk, New York, London: M.E. Sharp, 2005. xiii+449 pp.

Rumer E., Trenin D., *Zhao Huasheng. With an Introduction by R. Menon. Central Asia. Views from Washington, Moscow and Beijing.* Armonk, New York, London: M.E. Sharp, 2007. vii+224 pp.
Rywkin M., *Moscow's Muslim Challenge: Soviet Central Asia.* Armonk, New York, London: Collier, 1982. 186 pp.
Rywkin M., *Stability in Central Asia: Engaging Kazakhstan. A Report (with Policy Recommendations) on U.S. Interests in Central Asia and U.S.-Kazakhstan Relations.* New York: NCAFP, 2005. 25 pp.
Schatz E., *Modern Clan Politics: the Power of Blood in Kazakhstan and Beyond.* Seattle, London: University of Washington Press, 2004. xxvi + 250 pp.
Schwab G. D., Rywkin M., *Security and Stability in Central Asia: Differing Interests and Perspectives.* New York: NCAFP, 2006. 36 pp.
Starr S. F., *Clans, Authoritarian Rulers, and Parliaments in Central Asia.* Washington, D.C.: Central Asia-Caucasus Institute & Silk Road Studies Program, Johns Hopkins University-SAIS, 2006. 27 pp.
Starr F. S. E., *A Greater Central Asia: Partnership for Afghanistan and Its Neighbors. The Central Asia-Caucasus Institute and Silk Road Studies Program.* Washington, DC: Joint Transatlantic Research and Policy Center, 2005. 38 pp.
Svanberg I., *Kazak Refugees in Turkey. A Study of Cultural Persistence and Social Change.* Uppsala:Uppsala University Press, 1989. 211 pp.
Svanbeg I. (Ed.), *Contemporary Kazakhs. Cultural and Social Perspectives.* Richmond: Curzon Press, 1999. xi + 151 pp.
Weller R. C., *Rethinking Kazakh and Central Asian Nationhood. A Challenge to Prevailing Western Views.* Los Angeles: Asia Research Associates, 2006.
Weitz R., *Kazakhstan and the New International Politics of Eurasia.* Washington, DC: Central Asia-Caucasus Institute & Silk Road Studies, 2008. 189 pp.

AUF DEUTSCH

Dieter H. (Hrsg.) *Die regionale Integration im Zentralasien.* Berlin: DSIE, 1995. 382 S.
Grossler S., *Kasachstans schwieriger Weg in die Unabhangigkeit: ein Erfahrungsbericht.* Koln: BIOIS, 1993.
Gumppenberg M.-C. v., *Die sozioökonomische Entwicklung in Kasachstan: Eine Gefahr fur den jungen Nationalstaat?* Köln: Berichte des BIOST 26/2000.
Gumppenberg M.-C. v., *Kasachstans Regionen // Osteuropa.* Nr 1. 2001. S.27–45.
Gumppenberg M.-C. von., *Staats- und Nationsbildung in Kasachstan.* Opladen: Leske und Budrich, 2002. 231 S. (Forschung Politikwissenschaft; Bd.150).
Halbach U., *Islam und islamische Bewegungen in Zentralasien // Aus Politik und Zeitgeschichte (Bonn).* Januar 2002. Bd.3–4. S.24–31.
Hoffmann L., Bofinger P., Flassbeck H., Steinherr A. *Kazakstan 1993–2000. Independent Advisors and the IMF.* Heidelberg, New York: Physica-Verlag, 2001. 278 pp.
Kasachstan. Staat im Zentrum Eurasiens. Wostok Spezial // Wostok (Berlin). 2001. Nr 4. S.1–82.
Létolle R., Mainguet M., *Der Ararlsee. Eine Ökologische Katastrophe.* Berlin, Heidelberg: Springer, 1996. 517 S.
Nazarbajew N., *An der Schwelle zum 21.Jahrhundert. Übers. von G.Rieger und M.D.Drevs.* Nürnberg: Harnisch, 1997. 260 S.

Sapper M., Weichchsel V., Huterer A. (Hrsg.) *Machtmosaik Zentralasian. Traditionen, Restriktionen, Aspirationen.* Bonn: BPB, 2007. 648 S.
Schreiber D., *Kasachstan entdecken. Auf Nomadenwegen zwischen Kaspischem Meer und Altaj.* Berlin: Trescher Verlag, 2003. 499 S.
Strasser A. (Hrsg.), *Zentralasien und Islam.* Hamburg: DOI, 2002.
Ufer H., Meimberg R., Poser J.A., Schönherr S., Theuringer M. Kasachstan – Wirtschaft im Umbruch. Kasachstan – Wirtschaft in der Krise/ Kasachstan – Wirtschaft weiter im Abschwung. Kasachstan – wirtschaftliche Talsohle in Sicht. Kasachstan Wirtschaft und Reformen 1995. Kasachstan 1996 – Zwischen Stabilität und Stagnation. Kasachstan 1997 – Konsolidierung auf noch Schmaler Basis. Regionale Strukturbildungsprozesse. – München, Köln, London: Weltforum Verlag, 1992–1998 (IFO Studien zur Osteuropa und Transformationsforschung: Nr. 10–31).
Wittschorek P., *Präsidentenwahlen in Kasachstan* 1999. Discussion Paper Nr 38. Bonn: ZEI, 1999. 50 S.
Zukunftregion Kaspisches Meer. Deutsche Interessen und Europäische Politik in den transkaukasischen und zentralasiatischen Staaten. Positionspapier der SPD-Bundestagsfraktion. Bonn: Cicero, 1998. 47 S.
Zentralasien: eine Innenansicht. Berlin: FES, 2006. 498 S.

AU FRANÇAIS

Bennigsen A., Lemercier-Quelquejay Ch., *Les musulmans oubliés. L'Islam en Union Soviétique.* Paris: Maspero, 1981. 320 pp.
Blanchard L., *Le Kazakhstan // Ètudes et Conjoncture. Cahiers de l'INSEE.* 1961. No 5, pp. 405–487.
Carrère d'Encausse H., *La gloire des nations ou la fin de l'Empire soviétique.* 2e ed. – Paris: Fayard, 1991.
Cagnat R., *La rumeur des steppes. Aral, Asie centrale, Russie.* Paris: Payot et Rivages, 2001. 322 pp.
Chambre H., *Le Kazakhstan: tiers-monde soviétique? // Union Soviétique et développement économique. 2-me partie.* Paris: Aubier Montaigne, 1967, pp. 259–370.
Dore R. (ed.), *L'Asie Centrale et ses voisins.* Paris: Inalco, 1990.
Fourniau V., *Histoire de l'Asie Centrale.* Paris: Presses Universitaires de France, 1994. 128 pp.
Djalili M., Kellner T., *Géopolitique de la nouvelle Asie Centrale.* Paris: PUF, 2001. 585 pp.
Laruelle M. Peurouse S., *Les russes du Kazakhstan: identités nationales et nouveau États dans l'espace post-soviètique.* Paris: Maisonneuvre et Larose, 2004.
Nazarbaev N., *Sans droites ni gauches.* Lausanne: L'Age d'Homme, 1993. 225 pp.
Poujol C., *Le Kazakhstan.* Paris: Presses Universitaires de France, 2000. 128 pp.
Poujol C., *L'islam en Asie centrale vers la nouvelle donnée.* Paris: INALCO, 2001. 106 pp.
Poujol C., *Dictionnaire de l'Asie centrale.* Paris: Ellipses, 2001.
Poujol C., Gentelle P. (dir.) *Peuples des steppes en Asie centrale.* Paris: Autrement, 2002. 223 pp. (Collection Monde N° 132)
Raballand G., *L'Asie Centrale ou la fatalité de l'enclavement?* Paris: L'Harmattan, 2005. 360 pp.
Rashid A., *Asie Centrale, champ de guerres. Cinq républiques face à l'islam radical. Pastface de O.Roy.* Paris: Edition Autrement, 2002. 232 pp.
Roy O., *L'Asie centrale contemporaine.* Paris: PUF, 2001. 127 pp.

Index